Time Management Secrets
for College Students

TIME MANAGEMENT SECRETS FOR COLLEGE STUDENTS

The underground playbook for managing school, work, and fun!

Dennis Stemmle

College Success Academy
COLLEGE SMARTER NOT HARDER

Time Management Secrets for College Students

The underground playbook for managing school, work, and fun!

© 2019 Dennis Stemmle

ISBN-13: 978-0692197462 (Paperback)

Praise for Time Management Secrets for College Students

"Thinking of my situation in college, I feel like giving up. After reading this book, I have faith in myself and my ability to receive my degree. I just need to adjust to this environment. This was such a great book and is a great resource for all college students." –Candice Young, a student at Coastal Carolina University.

"This book spoke volumes to me. I needed this book at the beginning of the semester. The learning pyramid in college did change, and it took me a while to adjust. Phenomenal book overall." –Amber Jenerette, a student at Francis Marion University.

"This is the playbook for how to make yourself successful in college. Time Management Secrets for College Students is useful, practical, and vital. Highly Recommended!" –Dennis Coe, a student at the University of South Carolina.

"An absolute must-read for any student or parent seeking to ensure success in college." –Brayden Gisler, a student at North Carolina State University.

"I found Time Management Secrets for College Students to be very useful, and I will definitely be using some of these skills next semester." –Casey Mize, a student at Auburn University.

"Time Management Secrets for College Students gave me motivation, and I enjoyed reading this book!" –Zach Weisz, a student at Cal. State Fullerton.

"Very helpful, very encouraging, and very uplifting." –Davis Sims, a student at Murray State University.

"As a student-athlete, this book is my new bible! Super helpful to not just student-athletes but every college student. Great read!" – Jessica Fyock, a student at West Chester University.

"Every college student should read Time Management Secrets for Students! I recommend this book to all my peers." –Grayson Lymon, a student at UCLA.

"This book offers college students many skills that can be applied to their daily lives!" –Alfonsa Revas, a student at Arizona State University.

"I found a lot of the tips in this book to be very useful, especially the one about picking a major that opens up a lot of options in the future." –Emilee Russell, a student at Fredonia State University.

"Time Management Secrets for College Students gives me the motivation I needed to set goals for myself and know that I can achieve them if I believe in myself." –Susan Kamery, a student at Santa Monica College.

"I really enjoyed reading this book, and I am going to recommend it to my peers!" –Mohrgan Sokolowski, a student at Florida Atlantic University.

"This book made me realize how much I always procrastinate with everything, and it made me want to stop waiting around and start achieving my goals." –Noelle Anzivine, a student at Jamestown Community College.

"I really liked Time Management Secrets for College Students because it offered a lot of skills and tips that can be applied to my everyday life at school. It teaches the value of goal setting and ways to efficiently accomplish them! –Gabby Pfeiffer, a student at Arizona State University.

"Professor Stemmle has his finger on something here-something very important. Anybody interested in achieving academic success should embrace the approach outlined in Time Management Secrets for College Students." –Mary Sheehan, a student at the University of Massachusetts Amherst.

"Time management is one of my biggest downfalls as a college student and even harder to manage; this book helps me break down what I need to do to help be more successful in college! 10/10 would totally recommend!" –Erin Neal, a student at Coastal Carolina University.

"Time management is essential to excel during anyone's college career. This book provides all the critical secrets that can assist any college student." –Elisabeth Ranieri, a student at Temple University.

"This book really opened my eyes to a whole new way of time management thinking. After reading this book, I really can now understand where I'm going wrong and what I can do to improve." –Cammie Daniels, a student at West Chester University.

"Awesome read not just for college but for life in general. The secrets taught will help any person be successful." –Mala Neal –York College Grad, a student at Atlanta's John Marshall's Law School.

"Professor Stemmle outlined a clever approach to conquering success as a college student. I think many could benefit from reading this book." –Tom Connolle, a student at the University of Massachusetts Amherst.

"Time Management Secrets for College Students is a powerful system to catapult you to the top of your college class." –Molly Buring, a student at the University of South Carolina.

"A brilliant formula for achieving academic success in college. As a junior, I only wish I had this formula from the beginning." –Joseph Gisler, a student at East Carolina University.

"So glad I have read this! Time Management Secrets for College Students is a lifesaver for procrastinators and people with horrible time management skills like me!" –Abby Gregg, a student at Francis Marion University.

"Why am I now just reading this book? Professor Stemmle's Time Management Secrets for College Students is a book I should have read freshman year!" –Carly Ward, a student at Coastal Carolina University.

"This book has taught me so much about time management! Time Management Secrets for College Students is a must have for a college student of any age!!" –Casey Weaver, a student at Appalachian State University.

"My name is Steven Tobolski, and first off, I could not have been more satisfied to have Professor Stemmle as my Marketing teacher throughout my semester at Coastal Carolina. After reading his book, I now am on a better time managed track to opening my own business." –Steven Tobolski, a student at Coastal Carolina University.

"Before I read this book, the way I distributed my tasks throughout my very busy schedule was ineffective and messy. After I read this book, I gained very helpful tools to help execute my tasks with my very limited time." –Kenidy Springer, a student at Coastal Carolina University.

"Currently being a full-time college student and owning my own Roofing/Tree service business, it's super hard to manage my time. After reading *Time Management; Secrets for College Students*, it really helped me better my decision making and plan out my overloaded schedule." –Bryce Aulffo, a student at Coastal Carolina.

"A book that I will continue to read at the beginning of each semester as a reminder of what to do to be successful." –Austin Hernandaz, a student at Coastal Carolina University.

"Great read for a procrastinator! Time Management Secrets for College Students has tips I will keep and use for the rest of my life." –Nyela Jackson, a student at Coastal Carolina University.

"As a college student, I struggle with time management. This book, Time Management Secrets for College Students, has made me want to ensure my success in college and manage my time better." –Alec Mastroine, a student at Coastal Carolina University.

"This book absolutely changed the way I delegate my tasks throughout my very busy college schedule." –Austin Nicklas, a student at Coastal Carolina University.

"Professor Stemmle's book, Time Management Secrets for College Students, will give you the motivation to ensure your success as a college student." –Nicole Corsi, a student at Coastal Carolina University.

This book is dedicated to:

Those students who will not let their life be a shooting star that lights up the night sky for only a moment, but instead lives every day with real passion and purpose. Those students that learn to master the moment of decision and choose to be the best version of their self every day, not because it is easy, but because it is uncommon! For these students, better has no finish line! I admire your efforts, and I hope this book will provide encouragement, and be a tool that will make your journey easier.

Acknowledgments

When I first thought about writing this book, I wanted to be sure to acknowledge everybody who positively impacted my life and career. It is through others that I have gained my knowledge and experience that so powerfully contributed to me becoming the person I am today. I am eternally grateful for these mentors, coaches, and friends. This shared knowledge provided a foundation for any success I have been fortunate enough to achieve in my life.

To all the college students that provided feedback and insights on this project, I am grateful for the time you took to make this book better.

To my son Bradley who strongly encouraged me to share my thoughts and ideas with college students everywhere.

To my wife Karen, whose support has been endless.

Finally, a thank-you to the young men and women I have had the privilege to teach over the years. May you always choose to pursue the best version of yourself!

Contents

College Bound!

"Every new beginning comes from some other beginning's end." — Seneca

You've made that walk across the stage and collected your high school diploma, and immediately started dreaming of the freedom you'll enjoy in college! Congratulations! You're beginning a new journey sure to be filled with excitement, new experiences, and a host of new challenges and expectations. Some questions that might be running through your head include:

- How will I adjust to the college environment?

- How will I make new friends?

- Will I be able to succeed in this next phase of my life?

- Will I be stressed out all the time?

- How will I be able to get all the things done that are on my plate?

- How will I fit all my stuff into my small dorm room?

- Will I get along with my roommate?

- Will everybody be smarter than me?

- How will I be able to manage all my activities?

- Is it ok to feed the squirrels on campus?

- Will I miss my family and friends?

While all these questions are of extreme importance to most new college students, the key to pulling everything together and having a great college experience is establishing good habits. The foundation for forming good habits starts with a clear understanding of your goals and the development of an effective time management system.

At first, you will seem to have more time available to you than you will know what to do with. Even if you take a huge class load, have a part-time job, and sleep a lot, I guarantee that you are going to initially feel like you have more time than you initially imagined. This feeling is all a grand illusion and is the underlining reason why most students find themselves overwhelmed, depressed, and having to pull the dreaded all-nighters that everybody fears.

You see in college; it is not unusual for 40% to 50% of your grade to be earned in the last month of a semester. While you are cruising along with little care at the start of the semester, that last month is out there looming, waiting to reap havoc on your GPA. This last month effect is like a mountain that has accumulated snow over the winter months, a slight change in conditions can bring about an avalanche. What seemed like a manageable workload has now spun out of control, the avalanche is upon you.

Most college professors do want you to succeed, and they typically weigh early assignments less to help you get adjusted to their style and expectations and gradually increase the difficulty of the test and assignments as the semester progresses. Keeping with our snow analogies, this progressive ramping up in your coursework is like a snowball rolling down a mountain, gathering more snow and momentum as it goes. To avoid being overtaken by the snow, you will learn how to apply my strategies of breaking down your assignments into smaller chunks and creating milestones throughout the semester avoiding getting flattened by those proverbial snowballs.

Proper Time Management is all about breaking your assignments, tasks, and commitments into smaller chunks and then maximizing the time you have each day. You see, by working a daily plan, we never let those snowballs roll too far down the mountain, we keep them small and manageable, at any time we can bend over and pick one up and throw it wherever we want with little effort at all. When the unexpected happens, you get sick, a parent has a health issue, you must pull that extra shift at work, your buddy the squirrel has gone missing, you have kept life's snowballs manageable and within control. You would be shocked to learn the number of times a student has come to me and said they couldn't turn in a project they were supposed to be working on ALL semester because they had left their project to the very last week of the term and some life event happened. Even if that life event had not occurred, they would be lucky to pass the assignment given the hole they dug for themselves.

Time Management makes all the difference in succeeding in college, graduating on schedule, enjoying this time in your life or completely struggling and being stressed out and maybe, like 50% of students who enter college, completely dropping out altogether.

For many first-year college students, this experience is an extremely challenging transition. Your parents aren't around anymore to make sure you get up for school. You go from being a "big" senior to a "newbie" freshman once again. College is the beginning of your adult life. You will be learning what you need to know to succeed in the real world. That, alone, can be overwhelming!

But it doesn't have to be. One important key to success is learning proven time management skills to maximize your overall college experience. How do you do that? It's not always easy, but it will be easier – with the help of this valuable book (shameless plug alert).

Inside these pages are valuable tips to learn how to schedule your time efficiently, how to stop procrastinating, how to shut out distractions, and how to manage your studies and work with your personal life. A huge part of this experience is stress management, and I've provided many valuable tips and tricks to minimize stress and enjoy the whole college experience.

We all probably wish that there were more hours in a day, but since that is impossible, we must make the best use of the hours that we do have. By utilizing the information in this book, you will be well on your way to achieving better time management skills and becoming an all-around better college student. It doesn't matter if you're an 18-year-old freshman right out of high school, a senior almost ready to graduate, or a 35-year-old returning to classes for the first time in 15 years, these skills and ideas can apply to everyone. And, they will apply to your life after college as well! Learning effective time management skills makes life much easier and allows you more and more time for you to pursue the things that matter the most to you.

The Journey to Writing This Book

"Each day is a journey, and the journey itself is home." — *Matsuo Basho*

My wife Karen and I were sound asleep when we were startled by the vibration of her cell phone on the nightstand next to her. It was almost three am in the morning, and we had no idea who would be calling at this time, but we knew it was either a wrong number or unwelcome news as "nobody calls at this hour with good news."

On the other end of the phone was our son Bradley, and even though Karen had answered the phone and was speaking to him, I could hear the panic in his voice through her phone. As I heard his frantic voice over her phone, I got a shooting pain in my stomach, and I felt this wave of anxiety overcome me. I was hundreds of miles away, and our son was overcome with anxiety, fear, and stress. He was in full-blown panic mode; we were not sure why yet, which, led to an enormous feeling of helplessness. My palms started sweating, yet I felt my body temperature falling, and I was cold at the same time. As Karen tried to calm him down and figure out what was going on, I was becoming overcome with my fear and frustrations, wondering if he was ok, had he been hurt, just what had happened?

As it turned out, he had not been in an accident, gotten hurt, or fallen ill, he was having a panic attack driven by his complete feeling of being overwhelmed by his first semester of college. We were shocked by this turn of events. By all accounts, we thought everything was going well for him at school. He had communicated during the first few weeks of school that all was going well, had scored high on the ACT and made excellent grades in High School, and he was accepted into all the colleges he applied to. It just had never crossed our minds that he would ever struggle academically in college.

He explained how things just suddenly seemed to shift on him. He had an exam that was to take place, not in his regular classroom or building, but another location across campus. He underestimated the time it would take to walk over, and when he got there, he had difficulty finding the exam room. When he did find the room, he was 15 minutes late for the exam, and the professor would not let him take the test and informed him that he would receive a zero on that exam. The effect of that 15 minutes not only would rattle him mentally but would require him to ace every other assignment to even pass the class. At the same time, his other class initial exams were happening, and he bombed his freshman calculus exam. The combined impact of these events now had him behind the eight ball in two classes and would require him to make a significant time commitment and effort in these two classes.

With all the extra effort going into the two classes, he found he could no longer maintain his other grades. Subsequently, he failed a chemistry test, and now he had an issue in three classes. To gain a little more time to improve his grades he decided to skip a few classes where he was doing very well, and he relied on class notes from a friend. This strategy he reasoned would allow him to pull up his poor grades without impacting the classes he was doing well in. However, as he focused more on the classes he was struggling with, he paid less and less attention to his other classes, and his A's and B's had fallen to C's or D's.

His strategy was not working, his hard work was not working, for the first time in his academic career he was really struggling, he lost his confidence and he felt like every decision he was making was wrong, each mistake seemed to be compounding on the prior, and he had never experienced a struggle like this before. He did not know how to ask for help, he did not want to let anyone down, he was one of those kids where everything had just always come easily to him, and now it wasn't. He became swept up in the proverbial avalanche.

Panic had set in; he had lost all confidence in his decision-making abilities as he suddenly realized that the series of small seemingly minor choices he had made to fix things had the exact opposite effect. As silly as it may seem, he felt everything was crashing down on him, spinning out of control and he was completely overwhelmed. As Bradley laid in bed and thought about all his choices, the money spent, his fear of letting us down, his mind was racing, and he just panicked, he thought he could be having a heart attack, his heart was racing, his whole body was broken out in a sweat, so he called home in a panic.

Karen was able to calm him down, and explain to him what was going on with his body. She told him to meet with his advisor for some help and guidance, she let him know we loved him and it was all ok, he was not the first student to go down this road, and he would not be the last.

His guidance counselor recommended two potential courses of action. The first recommendation was that he could do a complete semester withdraw. A semester withdraw, sets the clock back to zero, and he would start over. The second option he presented was to drop a couple of classes allowing him a chance at salvaging part of the semester. He felt dropping two classes would enable him to recover, and although he passed his classes, he did end up his first semester with a GPA of 1.67 and found himself on academic probation.

As parents we felt helpless, we hated to see him struggle, see him stressed, feeling down on himself, and feeling like he was a failure. As a new college professor, I had always just assumed that my students who struggled academically had always struggled academically. I would learn that nothing was further from the truth.

I discovered that only around half of students who enroll in college actually end up graduating with a bachelor's degree! Tragically, one in four college freshman dropout after their first year and another third of students transfer before graduating, adding thousands of dollars to the cost of their degree. I also learned that less than 60 percent of students who enter four-year schools graduated within six years.

The system was not working! As a result of this broken system, students and parents were being left with thousands of dollars of student loans, mounting stress and piles of credit card debt, all with no degree or plan to help pay off these loans.

We were not alone! The problem had reached epidemic proportions, hidden in plain sight under the headlines of mounting student debt. It seems no one was peeling back the onion; everyone was focused on the obvious issue, growing tuition costs. Student success or lack thereof was an epidemic that universities and the media were not discussing! The real issue is that our education system is just not preparing our kids to transition successfully to college.

If you are like most folks, you assume good high school students will do well in college; you would be wrong. Also, if a student does well on their ACT or SAT there is no assurance that they will do well in college. In fact, study after study shows that there is little correlation between these standardized tests and college success. In fact, *researchers found that the composite ACT scores of students who graduated and those who dropped out were nearly identical - 24.5 and 24.1* points, respectively.

So, I asked the next logical question... If all the traditional measures of success cannot predict your success in college, what would? I knew there had to be a proverbial canary in the coal mine somewhere! **Then I found it!**

A paper, published in the *Journal of College Student Retention: Research, Theory and Practice* (everybody reads this one, right!). It turns out that the freshmen who persisted to graduation had significantly higher first-semester GPAs - 2.84 versus 2.20, respectively - compared with peers who left without earning a degree. **It was my Eureka moment - "First-semester GPA was the proverbial canary in the coal mine."**

But I needed to dig deeper. I needed to understand what made some students successful and other students with seemingly the same background unsuccessful. If I could find this answer, I knew Bradley could recover, but I needed to find out quickly!

In between semesters, Bradley came home, and we spent days going through his study habits, note taking approaches, how he prepared for a test, interacted with his professors and other students, how he approached time management, his sleep habits, social interactions, you name it, we looked at it. I researched all I could find online, read books, scholarly papers, and asked hundreds of college students for their tips, tricks, and insights into their challenges and how they overcame them. I noticed the same themes popping up repeatedly and time management was at the core. Utilizing this knowledge Bradley and I developed a plan. The underlying theme was quite simple; we needed to focus on the difference in environment between college and high school. The unstructured college environment requires a different game plan, a different approach to success then your structured high school experience.

9

Let me explain, in high school, students learn about 80% of the course material in class and 20% out of the classroom. In high school, many students learn if they attend class, cram the night before a test, prepare a paper or assignment a day or two before its due they can still make an A in their classes. In High School, a bell goes off you go to class, another bell goes off, and you go to another class, a bell goes off, you go to lunch. If you miss school, your parents get a phone call. The teachers will remind you when tests and assignments are due. It's all pretty straightforward and controlled.

In college, the structure goes away. The learning pyramid is flipped upside down. You do about 20% of your learning in class and about 80% of your learning out of class. In fact, it is not unusual for 40% to 50% of your grade to occur during the last month of the semester. You have projects, papers or other assignments that you are supposed to be working on all semester long. In college, you learn the hard way that you can't throw these assignments together the week before they are due and expect to make a good grade or even pass for that matter. And if you multiply this last month effect times the four or five classes you are taking; it becomes quite easy to understand how things can unravel even for the best students.

But things don't have to unravel on you. Everything we had learned and applied worked better than any of us could have imagined. Bradley went from a 1.67 GPA and academic probation his first semester, to a 3.9 GPA and the Dean's List his second semester. One B+ kept him off the President's List!

Best of all, the semester was virtually stress-free except for a spike during that crazy last month. But because he had a plan and system in place, his stress level was manageable, and his grades improved during that final month. He was expecting about a 3.6 GPA, and when that final month ended, and those big assignments, exams, and papers were graded, he had pulled a 3.9 GPA! All A's with one B+ (which was the result of one poor test, it will happen no matter how much you plan or how hard you work).   But more than the GPA, he regained his confidence, he was having fun again, and he had time to enjoy his college experience.   He was a completely different person, he was enjoying studying, learning, and working hard.

At this point, I realized I had two choices. My first option was to do nothing else. And if that were the end of the story I would be great, Bradley would be great, the system we developed was already working for him, but I realized there was a second option, an option that could allow me to help millions of other students and their families.

I realized this wasn't just about my family anymore; it was about yours. You see, the education system just isn't working for millions of students who are struggling to transition successfully from high school to college. Families and students are falsely led to believe that because they made good grades in high school and on their ACT or SAT, they are ready for college, and that is not true.   It is a terrible lie costing our economy billions of dollars each year and shattering the dreams of millions of students every year.

I want you to think about something for a minute… Don't you deserve every opportunity to become who you want to be? Don't you deserve to be prepared for your journey to college? Don't you deserve to learn from other people's mistakes, to stand on the shoulders of those that have gone before you? I think you do, and that is why I wrote this book. "Time Management for College Students" is a completely new way to demystify the complete college experience and give you every opportunity for the success that I know you so strongly desire and deserve.

You deserve to enjoy everything about college life - the education, parties, camaraderie, sporting events, and of course all those new friends. You can accomplish all this and not sacrifice the real reason why you're here – to ~~get a great job~~ for an outstanding education. I can show you how!

You have made a great decision in reading this book. I am so excited to help you get the most out of this time in your life. As you start this new journey, I don't want you to be alone. We have a group of your peers, all sharing this amazing journey together. You can join our community at Facebook.com/CollegeSuccessAcademy.

When you come, please take a picture of yourself holding this book, and post that picture in our group introducing yourself to our tribe and use the hashtag #CollegiateHacker in the post!

Thanks again for getting your copy of this book, and I can't wait to start telling your success story!

Dennis Stemmle

P.S. Never Forget... You Got This!

As a reader of this book, you can take advantage of more training at www.IwantSuccessInCollege.com.

Goal Setting for College Students

"If you want to be happy, set a goal that commands your thoughts, liberates your energy and inspires your hopes." — *Andrew Carnegie*

Goal Setting Made Simple

To get what you want from life, you first need to know what it is you want. After all, how can you fulfill your potential if you don't know where you want to go, who you are or what makes you happy?

Now, most of you are probably thinking I have no idea what I want to do with my life yet! That is more than ok and quite expected. Figuring out life's big questions takes time, and goal setting is such a crucial step in that journey. Learning how to properly use goals to get the most out of your life is a critical skill set to obtain. If you don't know what your goals are, then life becomes a little like going on a journey with no destination in mind. Even though you might enjoy the journey, you're still going to risk ending up somewhere you don't want to be, and you certainly won't take the most efficient route to get there!

Sounds simple, right? You have to ask yourself what you really want from life and then go and get it. Right?

Unfortunately, it's not. Regrettably, goal setting is anything but easy and is very much a skill in itself. The problem is that not many people realize this, and they never think to assess the quality of the goals themselves. They blame their motivation, their circumstances or even other people. But rarely do they assess whether the issue might be with their goals themselves.

What are your goals? Really, what are your goals? Do you want to make the Dean's List, discover your passion, land a job, skate by with any degree? Goals are important for everyone and identifying them up front helps you stay focused along the way.

Why set goals? Life is very unstructured and has a way of getting away from you. At any given moment, there are thousands of possibilities, new bright shiny objects, a new viral cat video, a few hundred social media posts from friends, and a host of other things you could do. When you prepared to get your driver's license, you took drivers education; you practiced hours on end, you learned the rules of the road. When you went for your driver's test the tester told you where to go, where to turn left, turn right, speed up, turn around, etc., you just did not hop in the car and decide to drive to Alaska to see some Kodiak bears and demonstrate your great driving skills along the way. But what is it that keeps you from ending up in Alaska? The answer is that you got into your car with a clear goal of getting that driver's license you had dreamed about for years! You knew at the beginning exactly what your goal was, and you had a clear plan, and you stayed focused on that plan.

Life is the same way. If you know at the beginning where you want to go, you'll probably get there. Even if detours and delays arise, eventually you'll get there. But if you don't know where you're going, you probably won't end up at a point that makes you happy.

But what if I don't know where I want to go? That's ok, at most universities your first two years are filled with a common core, your Math, English, Sciences, etc., set a goal for yourself to perform well in those classes. Work a few courses in that you think you might enjoy. Set a goal to pick a major after you have had time to explore some different opportunities. This approach will allow you to divide your goals into time frames (immediate goals, short-mid-term goals, and long-range goals). You don't have to have firm answers to those gripping questions about what you want to be or do when you're done at college to make this work; your goals are likely to shift and change over time anyway. All you need to do right now is think of a handful of goals to get started. Write down a list of goals now before reading further.

An Example of Bad Goal Setting

To understand how to write a good goal, it can help first to take a look at what makes a bad goal. Why is it that some goals don't work out the way they should? What should we do differently to avoid this happening the next time?

Let's imagine for a moment that you want to get into shape. You're planning on losing weight and building muscle – which is a pretty common goal that an awful lot of people are interested in accomplishing.

In this example, a typical goal might involve writing down the ideal body weight and measurements that you are trying to reach and then setting yourself a target – three months, six months or one year. And then you get to it! But, this is a goal that is destined to fail. Why? Because this goal it is far too vague, far too distant and far too out of your control.

Let's fast forward two weeks, at which point you have hopefully been training hard for a while and changing your diet. Suddenly, life starts to get in the way. You find yourself bogged down with other things you have to do like that upcoming exam, paper, or party on Friday night and you don't have the time or energy to make it to the gym today. Or tomorrow. And the day after that is looking shaky as well.

But you tell yourself it is okay because you don't need to work out. Not working out on those days is not breaking your goal. You have plenty of time to reach your goal, and it is up to you how you are going to go about making it happen. So, if you take time off today, you'll just put some more time in tomorrow. Or the next day. If this week is a write-off, then you can always make up for it next week.

And so, it continues, week after week, until you get to the end of your allotted time span and you realize you've blown any chance of accomplishing that goal.

Or how about this alternative scenario? Imagine that you did put in the time and you worked very hard every day to get into shape. But the pounds just didn't come off. Maybe this is due to a slow metabolism, maybe it boils down to those late-night snacks or just too much partying.

Either way, you get to a certain point, and you realize once again that you aren't going to make it even though you tried your best. So, what do you do? You give up, disheartened, and you quit trying.

A Better Goal

Now let's imagine that same scenario but this time we approach our goal differently. What would a good goal look like if you wanted to lose weight or build muscle?

For starters, you should remove the time element. Instead of aiming to accomplish something in X number of days, how about you instead aim to do something toward your goal every day. Look at the goal that you want to accomplish and then break that down into much smaller steps. To lose weight, let's say you need to eat 1,800 calories or less a day. And you need to work out three times a week for an hour each day. If you can stick to this plan, then you will eventually notice changes – be they big or small.

Instead of focusing on the end goal, set yourself a daily plan. A daily goal is something that is entirely within your control – meaning that you cannot "fail" for reasons outside of your control. It is also completely resistant to being put off or delayed. You can't "work out today" tomorrow! Likewise, a slow metabolism isn't going to prevent you from eating only 1,800 calories.

I learned this concept from actor/comedian Jerry Seinfeld. Jerry developed a technique that he uses to make sure he sticks to these kinds of goals, and he calls it "The Chain." The idea is that he builds a chain each day as he completes his daily goal, each day represents a new link in his chain, and this process creates an immense pressure not to break the chain. For Jerry, the process of writing one new joke each day allowed him to craft his skills and provided the foundation for his tremendous long-term success.

An easy way to implement this strategy is with a calendar and a pen. Every day that you successfully achieve 1,800 calories or less, you put a tick on the calendar for that day. Your daily tick marks will start to build up gradually, and over time, you will come to feel proud of that row of ticks, and not want to ruin it by missing one. You won't want to "break the chain."

Whether you use this approach or not, the point is that you should write goals that are immediate and simple. Meanwhile, you can let the overarching objective "take care of itself."

17

Is Your Goal Too Ambitious?

There's nothing wrong with an ambitious goal. Many people say that "dreaming big" can even make you more likely to accomplish your aim because it attracts attention, gravitates people toward you and helps get people on board. If you tell people you want to fly to space, you will get a lot more positive attention than if you tell people you want to climb Stone Mountain (a quartz monzonite dome formation just outside Atlanta, Georgia).

Therefore, another piece of advice that often gets thrown around is for you to "have visions, not goals." Visions are abstract, and they are grand. These are things you visualize and dream about, rather than things you write down and tick off. If you want to get into shape, then your goal can be to train three times a week, but your vision would be to become the best physical specimen you can – attractive to everyone and full of confidence and energy.

But while a vision can be as grand and extreme as you like, those smaller steps should still be small, and they should be easy. At least at the very start, your plan should be easy, and this will then allow you to build towards your higher overarching objective. Think of this as a pyramid. At the top, you have your grand vision for the future – something so exciting that it helps you to launch yourself out of bed in the morning. Beneath that, you might have your 'realistic' version of what you can achieve with your current resources. Beneath that, you might have the steps you are taking every day to achieve it.

The mistake a lot of people make is to lump all these things together and not to consider the necessary sequencing required to move from one level to the next. Lumping is the reason that someone who has never been to the gym before, might well write themselves a new training program that requires them to train for an hour a day, seven days a week and to do this on a diet of 1,000 calories. Is it any wonder that they don't tend to stick to their plan and fail to reach their goals?

Impatience is your enemy when it comes to writing good goals. People want to accomplish their goals now. They don't want to put in the time or the repetitious work that it takes to reach their goals. And they certainly don't want the fear that comes from the uncertainty that after all their work, they might not achieve their goals.

But you need to change that thinking. Everything worth having comes with work and diligence, and this is often highly repetitive and boring. If you want to get into shape, you need to train regularly, and it takes years to get to a point where your new physique is impressive and permanent. If you want to start your own business after college, well then there is a ton you need to learn before you even get going. Procrastinating on a goal is just as bad by the way – which is another reason it is so important you have a clear plan of action!

A good way to understand this process is to look at the world of video gaming. Video games begin with a few levels that are incredibly easy to prevent you as the player from getting discouraged quickly and quitting. Craft your goals the same way – if your "level one" is a massive, difficult battle, then you won't be successful.

Let's look at running. Lots of people get it wrong when they are taking up running for the first time. Here, they aim to start running long distances right away and losing weight. It's grueling, painful and unrewarding and it leaves them gasping and achy for days after.

What they should do is to first focus on getting good at running and on learning to like running. That means running short distances, not running too fast, not running too far and generally not pushing themselves beyond a sensible point. This way, they can gradually start to like running, and they can gradually find themselves running further and further without even trying.

Often, it only takes small changes to get to the place you want to be. The Japanese notion of "Kaizen" best exemplifies the impact of small changes. Kaizen essentially means lots of small changes that build up to significant results.

For instance, if you want to graduate with a 3.7 or higher GPA, then it might be easier to look at small changes you can make to get there, rather than massive ones.

- Go to class every day.
- Create note cards after each lecture.
- Make sure you get 7 hours of sleep every night.
- Commit to the use of your daily planner.
- Visit your professors during their office hours.

These are just a few small changes that should be easy enough for most students to stick to and yet they can be enough to impact your GPA total in your favor – eventually leading to cumulative GPA of 3.7 or better!

Take a look at your current goals. How many of the tasks that you intend to complete today contribute to accomplishing the goals you have set for yourself? Are you actively working on these goals? Are you procrastinating, putting key tasks off for a later time? What would you have to change about your life to make your goals a priority? What activities are taking you away from your goals? How can you eliminate or reduce these distractions?

Breaking your goals into manageable pieces can help. Once you have a set of goals, it is useful to decompose the goals into manageable steps or sub-goals. Decomposing your goals makes it possible to tackle them one small step at a time and to reduce any tendencies to procrastinate.

Consider for instance the goal of obtaining your college degree. This goal can be broken down into four sub-goals. Each sub-goal is the successful completion of one year of your program. These sub-goals can be further broken down into individual courses within each year. The courses can be broken down into tests, exams, term papers, etc., within the passage of the 16 weeks of classes in each semester. Each week is broken down into individual days, and each day into hours and minutes you'll spend in your classes and doing homework for each day.

While it may seem a bit overwhelming to think about all the activities that will go into earning that college degree, thinking of your goals in smaller chunks helps to reinforce the idea that there is a connected path linking what actions you take today and the successful completion and earning of your degree. Seeing these connections can help you monitor your progress and detect whether you are on track or not. Take some time now to think through the goals you've set and to break them down into their smaller constituent parts.

Pro Tip – Many students struggle with setting goals, and that is quite normal, you have your whole life ahead of you, and your goals will change. The idea here is to select goals that will give you the most options, open the most doors for you in the future. For instance, if all else is equal, a Marketing degree will give you more options then a degree in Ancient Animal Bite Marks. When in doubt, when uncertain, choose the path that gives you the most future options.

Now that you have made a list of goals, I want you to pre-experience them in your mind by visualizing the steps you will take to achieve your goals. Visualizing the steps you will act on to obtain your goals increases the probability of actually achieving your goals. Successful athletes pre-experience over and over in their minds how they are going to perform in a game, so they can be at their peak effectiveness once game day arrives. You can take the pre-experience from athletes and directly apply the method to any goal you want to achieve.

One mistake many students make in seeking a goal is that they can focus so much on reaching the goal, the end state reward, that they fail to enjoy their college experience. Many students are in such a hurry to graduate and start their careers that they don't get the most out of this time in their lives. We enjoy life more when we find satisfaction in our immediate efforts rather than thinking how nice it is going to be when we finally arrive at our distant goal.

For example, we enjoy a road trip more if we decide to take an interest in the landmarks along the way rather than just enduring the ride until we arrive at our destination. Similarly, we enjoy a class more if we explore the content beyond what is required rather than doing the bare minimum to pass the class.

Don't make the mistake of setting unrealistic goals or having so many goals that it is impossible to reach them. Students frequently do this at the beginning of the semester. They soon become discouraged when they realize they have neither the time nor the energy to accomplish all of their goals. Recognizing our physical, mental and emotional limits is an important component to realistic goal setting, and college is more than just getting that diploma.

Changing Your Mindset

While some people are almost certainly going to be jealous as you start achieving your goals, your biggest obstacle is likely to be yourself. College students are often their own worst enemy, and for some reason, whenever we start to become successful, some primal defense mechanism kicks in, and our mind starts telling us all these crazy things – which we usually believe because, hey, we are a bit scared and afraid.

The truth is, we doubt just about everything along the path to success. Successful people are the ones who have tricked their minds into being supportive rather than critical, and although it takes some practice, you really can change your mindset so that you can get out of your own way. Here are some ways that you can make sure you have the right attitude as you chase down your dreams.

1. **Believe in Success**: One of the things that we all do from time to time is to convince ourselves that for some reason, we don't deserve to be happy. Maybe it comes from feelings of guilt or perhaps just a lack of conviction that we're worthy of being happy and achieving our goals. Whatever the reason, if your mind is telling you that you don't deserve the kind of success you're hoping for – remind yourself that storyline is a lie. Believe that you deserve success and happiness. We all deserve it, but few people are willing to do what it takes to get it.

2. **Develop Confidence in Yourself:** You probably have heard the expression "Whether you think you can, or you think you can't...you're right." Confidence is a powerful thing, and when you have it you are almost unstoppable, but when you lack it, it can be hard to accomplish anything. You truly can achieve your goals. You have the brains, the energy, the attitude, and the ability. You have every tool that you need to fulfill every single one of your desires. You need to do the work; the belief will follow.

3. **Avoid Thinking in Extremes:** Thinking in extremes – both positively and negatively – can become one of your biggest obstacles in life. We tend to think in very polarizing terms, up/down, on/off, success/failure, happy/sad, etc. Of course, none of these extremes are absolute, but it is hard to be objective about the full range of outcomes when you're

standing right on the edge of something. Don't fall into the trap of thinking in extremes about your success or failures.

4. **Don't Overgeneralize**: Sometimes we all can be drama queens when something bad happens. We say things like "Oh, I'll never be able to achieve this goal." Negative thought processes are one of the worst mistakes you can make. Saying things like: "I must be the worst person ever to try this, I am not smart like other students." is a recipe for a long and difficult life. Setbacks are going to happen, and sometimes you are going to fail. It's not the end of the world, and you're probably doing better than a lot of people. Don't overgeneralize, try to look at things objectively and most importantly, keep going.

5. **Celebrate Your Success:** When you reach one of your daily, weekly, monthly or yearly goals, don't minimize it. Achieving any goal is a big deal. Every single time you reach a goal – even if it's nothing more than your daily progress update – you are building momentum. Keep going, keep meeting those goals because before you know it, you'll be achieving your dreams.

6. **Stop Believing Your Inner Idiot:** At times, we all allow negative thoughts to enter our minds and somehow, we will start to believe these thoughts – or at minimum we start to behave in a manner that supports these negative thoughts until such time something happens to change that negative belief – and that is a sure way to lose your motivation. For example, suppose you have a calculus class this semester. Before you have even walked into the class, sat thru a few lectures, or read the first chapter, you might have convinced yourself that there is no way you will do well in this class. The class is just too hard, and you will probably end up lost by the end of the first week, you'll be pulling all-nighters to have any chance to pass …you get the idea. It's okay to think about what might happen

in the future, but you have no idea what it holds, so don't convince yourself that you're a clairvoyant. You aren't.

7. **Stop Thinking Perfection:** You aren't perfect. You're never going to be perfect. No one on this Earth is perfect, and if you compare yourself to that standard, you are going to be the loser every time. Just accept that you are going to fail some of the time and when you do, learn from it and move on. It's perfectly okay to strive for perfection as long as you never expect perfection. Each day strive to be the best version of yourself that you can be but don't expect that version to be perfect.

Goals A Final Thought

As you can see, learning to structure your goals correctly and having the right mindset can make a big difference when it comes to your likelihood of accomplishing your goals. The key is to set your sights high but to have concrete, small steps that you can take along the way to get there. Don't focus on how long it is going to take, deal with it being "boring" and focus on repeating the same few actions every day until you eventually achieve the thing you want to achieve or become the person you want to become.

If you assess the situation in the future after you have gained more experience and knowledge, you can rethink your approach again. Like anything else, this approach takes time, practice and effort. In time, you will find things that work for you, and things that don't work. You should make adjustments to your process as you gain more knowledge and experience!

Now that you have your goals in mind, the next step is walking the road toward achieving them. Achievement begins with understanding our time. Let's explore how to become aware of the time you have available to you.

Small Changes... Big Impact

"Small, Smart Choices + Consistency + Time =
RADICAL DIFFERENCE" — Darren Hardy

Where Did My Day Go?

Have you ever looked at the time and thought wow it's 3:00 pm already, where did my day go?   We have all been there at one point or another, but the first key to managing your time is to understand where your time gets spent. One very helpful way of determining where your time goes is to start tracking your time. The process here is similar to making a schedule, but it works in reverse. Instead of writing things down that you are planning to do, time logging is a process of writing down the things that you have already done. Doing this is sort of a get-to-know yourself exercise because this practice will highlight many of the habits that you might not even realize are eating big chunks of your time.

For instance, some people find that every time they plan to do some classwork, they end up watching a YouTube video or two before starting on their work. That five or ten minutes a day can add up to days of lost study time over the course of just one semester. Instead of studying for that English test, they check their social networks and update their friends that they will be offline a few hours, which of course leads to a few quick interactions from well-wishing friends. Other people can't seem to find the motivation to get started, to find their focus and they find ways to procrastinate endlessly until the very last-minute when anxiety finally fuels action.

Whatever your current time management habits, time tracking will help you adjust and fine-tune your time management practices. Having accurate information about your time usage patterns is the foundation for forming good time management habits. The following are a few of my favorite recommendations to help you track your time. Please don't skip this exercise, take the time to do this – it will truly open your eyes and help you take control of your time.

1. Time tracking is not as complex as it might first seem. At the end of every hour make a note about how you spent your time for that hour. The note needn't be long - one sentence or less should suffice. If how you spent your time doesn't match an already planned activity, enter a comment as to what you did during that time. This way you will be able to review patterns that emerge in your use of time and make adjustments to improve your productivity.

2. Many people find it helpful to modify their planning page to facilitate tracking time. The modifications are easy enough: make two columns on your paper for each day of the week. In one column, write down the activity you are trying to achieve; in the second column, make notes on what you did with your time. The side-by-side comparison is very revealing and an excellent way to figure out where you're not using time in the way you intend.

3. Another effective way to make changes and get results from your time management strategies is to summarize your time use by a time category such as sleep, study, work, travel, etc.

27

Before doing the summary, make a sheet with different columns for each category. Your log sheet might look something like this:

Activity	Expected Time	Actual Time	Variance
Study for Math Test	3-hours	5-hours	-2 hours
Review English Notes	2-hours	1-hours	+1 hour
Read Book Chapter	1-hour	1-hour	0 hours
Work on Industry Paper	2-hours	3-hours	-1 hour
Group Study Session	2-hours	1-hours	+1 hour
Sleep	8-hours	5-hours	+3 hours
Night Out	4-hours	7-hours	-3 hours
Total	**22 hours**	**23 hours**	**-1 hour**

Estimate the amount of time that you think you spend on the various activities listed and enter these in the "expected" row of the summary sheet. Feel free to add any additional categories that might be helpful. Then log your time for one week on an hour by hour basis. When the week is over, summarize your time by category for each day, add up the values for all seven days of the week, and write the totals in the "actual" row of the summary sheet.

Summarizing your time use allows you to understand how much time you spend in the various areas of your life. It is almost certain that you will see a notable difference between the number of hours you expected to use in certain categories and the actual number of hours you spend.

If you find that you spend more time in one area than you wanted, and less in another, the weekly summary of time used indicates which activities to reduce to find the extra time you want for that neglected area of your life.

The differences between your expected use of time and your actual use of time represent your opportunities for improvement. These differences are where your focus should be. You need to identify and adjust the patterns in your behavior that are creating these variances. Small changes can make an enormous impact over time and greatly aid you in reaching your goals. These small changes when taken together drive a compound effect allowing you to achieve huge rewards from a series of small, but intelligent choices.

The reason this approach goes relatively unnoticed by the masses is that these small changes seem to make no immediate impact, no obvious impact, they don't seem to matter. Most people can't understand the cumulative effect that these small positive changes can create in their lives, they miss that these seemingly minor adjustments taken consistently over time will create significant differences. Let me give you a few examples of the power of small actions compounding over time featured in Darren Hardy's Bestselling book, The Compound Effect.

The Magic Penny

If you had a choice between taking $3 million in cash today or a single magic penny that would double in value every day for the next 31 days, which choice would you pick? If you've heard this parable before, you know the magic penny is your most profitable choice. But why is it so difficult to believe choosing the magic penny is the best choice in the long run? The basic reason is that we are programmed to believe that it takes large significant actions to make any difference in our lives. Also, our brains believe anything that takes long periods of time to deliver a result is painful and pushes us in the direction of immediate fun and gratification. Fun always seems to trump long-term commitment. Let's look at our magic penny example.

For the sake of discussion, let's say you took the $3 million in cash and your friend decides to take a flyer on that magic penny. On Day Seven, your friend has sixty-four cents. You, however, still have $3 million, less, of course, some of those fancy purchases you made. On Day Fourteen, your friend is up to a whopping $81.92. Not looking too good for your friend at this point! You have been enjoying your millions and watching your friend struggle with only pennies to show for it.

After 21 days, with only ten days left in our story, the magic penny has only generated $10,486. For all your friend's sacrifice, she has barely more than $10,000. You, however, have been enjoying a $3 million windfall. On Day Twenty-Seven the magic penny has only generated a poultry $671,088, you are thrilled with your decision to take the $3 million. But, then the seemingly poor performing magic penny starts to gain steam and the power of the compound effect starts to take hold. That same power of that seemingly ill-advised doubling magic penny, that small doubling each day takes hold and makes that magic penny worth $10,737,418.24 on Day Thirty-one, more than three times your $3 million.

What do you think about your choice now? This parable is meant to demonstrate the power of small actions taken consistency over time is surprisingly powerful. On day Twenty-nine, you've got your $3 million; the magic penny has about $2.7 million. It isn't until that 30th day that your friend pulls ahead, with $5.3 million. And it isn't until the 31st day that your friend blows your doors off; she ends up with a whopping $10,737,418.24 compared to your now seemly small $3 million.

Very few things are as powerful as the "magic" of compounding actions taken consistently over time. Not surprisingly, this "magic-force" is equally powerful in all areas of your life.

Better choices, reinforced with positive habits, applied consistently over time is the key to happiness and success in life. The sooner you realize that the habits that drive your actions are compounding your life into either success or failure, happiness or stress, and frustration. The good news is that tiny, small adjustments applied to your daily routines can dramatically change your trajectory and lead to the success you desire in your life. Once more, I'm not talking about massive quantum leaps of change or a complete renovation of your life. Just like the magic penny, seemingly minor changes can and will transform everything.

The Lost Plane

Another illustration of how a seemingly minor unnoticeable change can impact your goals is the story of an airplane traveling from Los Angeles to New York City. If the plane is a mere one percent off course leaving Los Angeles, with no course corrections in route, the plane will ultimately end up about 150 miles off target, arriving either in Dover Delaware or Upstate in Albany, New York. Just like a small one percent error leads to the plane missing its intended goal, so it is with your habits. One single poor habit, which doesn't look like much on the surface, can ultimately lead to you finding yourself miles from your goals and dreams.

For those of you now freaked out by the thought of not knowing exactly where you spend your time, here's something to consider. We all have 168 hours available in a week. Studies report that fully half of those 168 hours – 84 hours - are used up for the "basics" like sleeping, eating, showering, etc. How do your numbers compare to these estimates? How will you spend those critical remaining 84 hours per week?

Time Management 101

"Time = life; therefore, waste your time and waste of your life, or master your time and master your life." — Alan Lakein

As a college freshman, you have no experience in planning for your out of class coursework.   A good rule of thumb is to schedule two to three hours of schoolwork outside class for every hour of class time. Yes, this means for a full-time student with five classes, a traditional fifteen-hour class load per week, would have a recommendation of between thirty and forty-five hours of study/homework time each week.

Sure, this is a lot of time, especially if you breezed through high school on a lot less. This estimate reflects the time it takes to learn effectively at the college level typically. The estimate is a general guideline it's not a set-in-stone rule. Based on the difficulty of each of your classes you can adjust your planned times up or down as needed. As I previously stated, in high school about eighty percent of your learning was done in school and only twenty percent outside of school. In college, the ratio is now reversed creating a new challenge for you as a college student.   You only do about twenty percent of your learning in class, and eighty percent of your learning occurs outside of class.

This change from a very structured high school environment to a highly unstructured college environment requires a completely different approach to your academic career.   The key here is that you set aside this time exclusively for studying and then adjust based on your experience and results.

If you work a job and doing so isn't necessarily counterproductive to success at school, you'll need to consider your work schedule and make sure to plan some time for yourself each week. A starting point might be something like ten percent of your week or seventeen hours. What is more important than the specific targets are that you spend enough time on schoolwork to ensure that you're successful and that you spend enough time outside of school to ensure that you have a healthy balance.

Make sure you allow for unanticipated interruptions in your daily schedule. Leave some empty spaces during the day allows you to be flexible enough to handle interruptions or unexpected demands on your time that will happen. If the unexpected does not happen, time is available to do something else.

Many students find that if they schedule homework earlier in the day, they are less likely to be interrupted by unexpected events. Homework should be a part of each day's schedule. Students who participated in a major study on stress reported doing homework as the most frequently used method for reducing stress in their lives.

That might sound odd to you, but by staying ahead of the curve and keeping homework done, your stress levels will be lower because you won't have that activity hanging over your head constantly.

Remember that your daily schedule should include at least some time for doing what you want to do rather than just a long list of "have-to-dos." Looking forward to something each day is good for our mental health and can help prevent the feeling of burnout.

Some days may feel overwhelming when we look at our schedule. If this is the case, it is helpful to concentrate on one thing at a time and avoid looking at the whole day. You will be amazed at how quickly you will complete the tasks of the day.

Inevitably, you will need to make adjustments to your plans and your time management habits. As you encounter time troubles, keep in mind that some are predictable, some are not; some are controllable, some are not. For those that are not controllable, keep your cool and get back on track as soon as possible. For time troubles that you can control, and particularly those that occur routinely, deal with them directly and quickly so that they don't prevent you from achieving your goals.

Time management requires self-management. It takes time, but after a short period of self-management, time-management becomes an everyday habit.

- Pay attention to how you spend your time.

- Do not procrastinate on chores to be done.

- Do not leave assignments and projects until the last minute.

- Schedule enough time in the day for doing things you enjoy and for eating and sleeping. Lack of sleep is an epidemic problem on most college campuses.

- Use your time wisely. If you take the bus or shuttle, plan to catch up on your reading while traveling.

One of the best time management strategies is staying one day ahead. I'm sure some collective groans meet this statement, but I promise that staying exactly one day ahead of your classes will make your life much easier, especially when that bug that is circulating campus knocks the wind out of your sails.

At the beginning of most of your classes, your professors probably will give you one of the most important pieces of information you will ever receive -- the syllabus. In high school, you probably never received a syllabus. You didn't know what the reading assignment or homework assignment was going to be in two weeks. In college, you do. Why is this important? It is the key to taking control of your time.

Let's say it's the very first day of class. You get your syllabus for your biology class. In most cases, the first day of class is a no-brainer -- often a material lecture doesn't happen because the professor knows that a lot of people are going to drop/add classes that first week. You eye your nifty syllabus and see that the next class period will be a lecture over the first chapter of your $199.99 textbook. At this critical juncture, you may think:

"Wow, I already know what I'll be doing next class period. I wonder if this is really valuable information? Could I use this to my advantage?"

Many students ignore the golden ticket of the syllabus, stuff it into their backpack, make a paper airplane, or find some other creative use for these sheets of paper and do nothing until next class period.

When the next class period arrives two days later, you haven't read chapter one, but who cares, because your professor is going to talk about it. You figure that you will use the time-honored tradition of taking notes in class. After all, everyone's doing it.

But if you're spending all of your time trying to copy PowerPoint slides or copy written words on the board (your professor will most likely have handwriting that resembles some ancient language), you simply aren't going to absorb the material in most cases.

Let's say you take some great notes - good for you! Then you take the notes, which have all of the information you will ever need, and you put them in your folder, binder, backpack, or saddle-pack, and leave them there until the next lecture. Then you take more notes, add them to the pile, and soon you have lots of notes. Whoopee.

Before you know it, you have a test or quiz approaching, so you assemble your nifty notes and start restudying them like mad. You have to set apart a large chunk of time out of your schedule to review this old information so that it will be fresh in your mind for the test.

There is a better way. Now, let's pretend that you decided to get one day ahead. After your first-class period (and I know this is hard to do because during the first week there's so much fun to be found and so little work to do), you have a heart-to-heart with yourself and decide that you are going to get one day ahead.

If today's Monday, and the next class is Wednesday, you set aside some time on Monday afternoon or anytime on Tuesday and read the first chapter. You may even decide to take some notes, highlight, or even make notecards for definitions (more on notecards later).

When you walk into class on Wednesday, and your teacher starts talking, you have at least some idea and understanding around the lecture. You don't have to copy down definitions you've already read because you know they are in the book -- you remember reading them. Instead of frantically trying to copy notes like your poor confused classmates, you can relax and make a small tick mark to denote what the professor discussed and listen to what the professor is saying.

The lecture becomes your review session, and then you are in a much better position when test time comes. If the professor starts talking about something that you don't remember reading in the textbook, make certain to take good notes. The topic is either not covered in the book (so you can guarantee the professor will put it on a test), or it's something that you didn't quite absorb the first time you read it.

If you can do this for each of your classes at the very beginning of school, you will be in great shape. Once you get one day ahead, you can work at the same pace as everyone else, but always be a day ahead. Lectures will not be "note cramming sessions"; they'll be pseudo-reviews.

The toughest part is not getting lazy and letting that one-day buffer disappear. You can't let yourself slip behind because you know you're ahead. Once you lose that day, it's much, much harder to get it back in the middle of the semester because the pace of your classes will be picking up. If you can get ahead in that first week, the load will be much lighter.

Of course, there are exceptions to every rule. Not every class is equal in difficulty, and it may be extremely hard to get that one-day edge in certain classes that are complex, or in classes that depend almost 100% on lecture material that doesn't come from a text book.

Some classes may be just plain hard, and if you can't get a day ahead in one or two classes, that's fine. The time that you save by being ahead in your other classes will help you enormously in that tough calculus class you're taking.

If you find that reading your book is not helping you grasp the material, then talk to your professor. If they learn that you are trying to stay a day ahead, besides the inevitable brownie points that will follow, they will be willing to help you out. Professors are generally willing to bend over backward for any student that is putting out a serious effort to succeed in their class.

Let me mention that you may have some classes in which the professor has put together a "notes packet" that does contain copies of all the presentations and notes for that class. Be very careful not to depend solely on these notes as this could be a trap. Don't let those notes become an excuse to get lazy. Don't think that the class lecture doesn't matter because you have all the material, get one day ahead in the class notes, and again, all of the lectures will be your review sessions.

Pro Tip - Before arriving on campus, check your school's online portal to see if any of your professors have uploaded their syllabus. Some professors may expect you to come prepared to work day one and may have already given you an assignment.

All these approaches will not guarantee your success at college. That's because everyone learns differently. Try some of these approaches and see what works for you, what doesn't, what needs to be modified. Also, please visit CollegeSuccessAcademy.com for more insights, recommendations, and training for college success. With that said, proper time management will have you well down the road to success with more time to enjoy your college experience than if you went down the traditional trial and error process of just plain winging it day to day.

Putting the System into Action

Keeping a calendar is pretty straightforward, but surprisingly I have discovered most students don't keep one their first semester or two. If they do keep one, it is usually just a class schedule with locations, so they know when and where to go until they get their routine committed to memory.

I am going to offer you some advice that seems counter intuitive and conflicts with what most experts will tell you. First, let me say I am a fan of technology and using your Outlook, iPhone or Google Calendar as a way to track your activities as most experts recommend, but I want this to be your secondary source of scheduling, not your primary.

I recommend the use of an Excel Spreadsheet, a DayMinder GC520 or similar planner, and your automated calendar during your first two semesters. I know this might sound like overkill, but the idea here is not entering events and assignments into a calendar, but to develop a system that keeps you organized and on track.

After a couple of semesters, you will find the system and the process will have become a habit and will be natural for you.

Let's look at how all these approaches work together, and everything will become clear.

First Day/Week of the Semester

The first thing I want you to do is to take your syllabi from each class and markdown (in pencil) all your assignments for the semester in your DayMinder, don't forget mid-term and final exams).

Now use different color highlighters for each class (Math, English, Communications, etc.) and highlight your assignments in your planner.

Next, identify areas where you have multiple assignments, test, exams, etc. all clustered together in a particular week or day. These clusters allow you to see clearly up front where you are going to be stressed and have little time. If you are like most students, you will see a convergence around spring and fall breaks and the last month of the semester. Take a deep breath and don't panic!

Now we want to pay attention to the weights of our assignments. Review your syllabi for each class and underline in red in your planner all your significant assignments. Significant is a subjective term, and each class will vary, but in general, anything that is weighted 10% of your grade or higher will qualify.

Once we have our core class schedule, we have to make some study estimates. Use two hours of study time for each hour of class time as a baseline requirement for scheduling your week. Adjust this baseline up or down based on your comfort with and the difficulty of your class material. If you struggle with Math, you should bump up your baseline to 3 hours. If you are an English expert, you can adjust the baseline down to 1 hour or maybe 1.5 hours. We now want to schedule our study time right into your planner. Planning a specific study schedule is key to avoiding procrastination. If you work or play sports and have that weekly commitment, schedule it now. Keep track of your study and assignment hours, so that you can make adjustments throughout the semester.

Things are probably starting to look pretty crowded at this point, and you are beginning to wonder where all that free time you heard about is going to show up. Don't worry, by planning you will maximize your free time.

Now we want to identify the areas on your calendar where you have little or no assignments due. Highlight these areas in Green in your DayMinder. These are the areas we are going to utilize to pull forward work you previously underlined in red, and the areas where you have lots of things converging. Look for those large significant assignments and break them down into smaller chunks with new due dates you create for yourself, these are called milestones. By utilizing these green areas, you will balance your workload ensuring you reduce future stress and have the time available to do your best work.

If you know you are going to go out with your friends on Friday and Saturday nights, make sure you schedule that time as well. If you are going to be out to the early morning hours and then sleep in until 2 pm, plan for that. Be realistic and don't set yourself up to fail by scheduling 4 hours of study time every Saturday morning when you already know you will be sleeping until early afternoon.

Now that we have everything organized and scheduled, we can enter everything into our online or smartphone calendars and set up our alert notifications. The electronic calendar now keeps us on schedule, but our pre-planning ensures we effectively utilize our time.

I recommend that students get one day ahead in their classes as soon as possible, things happen, schedules change, etc., but by building in a day buffer, you are preparing for that unplanned event that will inevitably occur at some point during the semester.

Also, class syllabi are guidelines, and the due dates and assignments will change in many instances. You will want to make sure you prepare for that new last-minute paper the professor decided to throw at you the last month of classes. Yes, it happens more often than you will like. A professor will feel that the class isn't picking up on something as a whole or that something new has happened in the field, and the professor will decide to add an assignment to strengthen your academic foundation. He or She may feel like the class has not engaged or participated as well as they should have, or they may want to give everyone an opportunity to improve their grades. Regardless, you want to be prepared.

Also, schedule a time to Skype or call your family, or someone else important to you back home. You will be surprised at how fast the days can run together, and although you are probably texting frequently, your loved ones love to hear your voice and see your face.

Here a link to a free template you can download and customize to keep your self-organized and on track.

http://collegesuccessacademy.com/index.php/schedule/

This template is very straightforward and easy to use and will summarize all your activities for you in one place (see table 1). You merely enter your activities on the Class List and Activities Tab (see table 2) classes, study time, practices, clubs, events, etc., in the tab and the spreadsheet will organize everything for you.

Table 1: Time Management Schedule

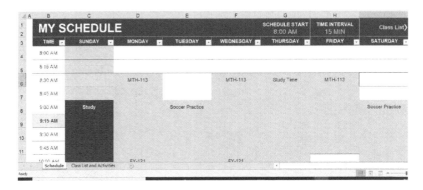

Table 2: Time Management Activities

Each Week – Review and Plan

Pick a day each week to review the week and month ahead. Most students find Sundays work best for this review. Remember to schedule calendar review time and treat this time like you would any other required commitment. Log into your universities course management system (we use MOODLE at CCU) and review your upcoming assignment lists for any changes or assignments you may have missed. As a side note, make sure you confirm all assignments you turned in are showing as turned in. Every semester students think they turned in an assignment, but the system will say otherwise. It is your responsibility to make sure your assignment was submitted and received. Use this time to clean up your email inbox and check and see if any of your professors have made schedule changes for the week ahead. The critical activity in this weekly review is to establish the specific activities and work you will perform during your allotted time slots. Initially, we just blocked off the time we knew we would need, once we have the specifics, we can now schedule the activities and tasks we need to complete during the week. As an example, we can take the 3 hours we have scheduled to study for a particular class and break down how we are going to use those three hours. Are we going to review note cards, read a chapter in the text, work on a paper, etc.?

Daily

Each day before noon, review your next day's schedule and school email account. If something new has popped up, you forgot about something, etc., by checking the next day's activities and your email early enough, you leave yourself time to course correct if needed. Many students check their next day's calendar just before going to bed, if they have made a mistake or missed something, they have no time to correct their error, stress levels rise, they don't sleep, and the next day's performance suffers. Students often don't get emails sent to their university accounts regularly, so they can get out of the habit of periodically checking their school email and can miss valuable information such as assignments or cancellations of classes.

The Big Picture

Most students struggle with structure, and that is natural. By creating a schedule, you are not somehow magically sucking all the fun out of your life. In fact, you are reducing your stress and improving your performance which will allow you to enjoy yourself a whole lot more. You will miss study sessions and other events on your calendar... that's ok. It is very valuable to know you missed an event and not go around fooling yourself into thinking you are on track. If you miss something, ask if you can make it up. You would be surprised how many students just assume the professor will not cut them a break. Make sure you identify what caused you to veer off course, make adjustments, and learn from the experience.

Creating Balance in Your Life

With everything that is going on in college, you need a simple system to make sure you have time for school, work, and fun. Yes, you're in college to get an education and to gain the skill you need for a successful career, but you also are here to have fun, create new experiences, and hopefully, a few lifelong friends.

There is a very simple technique you can use to make sure you keep your life in balance, a technique called *The Eisenhower Matrix or Eisenhower Box.* By utilizing this prioritization approach, you will be able to balance your hectic college life.

This technique is named after former President Dwight D. Eisenhower who was the top general in World War II. He is credited with many accomplishments in his life including leading the allied forces to victory, the development of the Interstate Highway System and spearheading the creation of NASA. As a General and a President, he was widely regarded as extremely effective and organized. We all can learn a lot from President Eisenhower, so let's take a look at how he was able to accomplish so much.

President Eisenhower was famous for saying "What is important is seldom urgent, and what is urgent is seldom important."

The matrix consists of a square divided into four sections or quadrants. Here's how the four quadrants are laid out:

We start by placing all our activities into the four quadrants, with the labels of Important and Urgent on each side. Each quadrant has a value of 1 through 4 based on their current priority.

1. **"Important" and "Urgent" tasks.** These are all your level 1 priorities. If you have an exam the next day, studying is probably a top priority. Paper due tomorrow, again, a level 1 activity, connect assignment due tomorrow, another level 1 priority. Level 1 priorities are those things with immediate deadlines, things that will make the most impact on your goals and vision, and these activities should grab your immediate attention.

2. **"Important," but "Not Urgent" tasks.** These are things still aligned with your goals and vision, but there is no immediate deadline staring you in the face. Maybe it is doing some extra reading on a topic in your major or attending a seminar before graduation or reviewing your 4-year plan. You will work these tasks whenever you have a lull in your schedule.

3. **"Not Important," but "Urgent" tasks.** These are things that you will complete after your level 1 priorities are complete or delegate altogether. Can your roommate check out that journal from the library for you? Could a friend pick up your toothpaste from the store for you? Maybe your parents need some information from you, or a friend needs a little help?

4. **"Not Important" and "Not Urgent" tasks.** These are the activities you put in quadrant 4 or activities you should eliminate altogether. Do you really need to binge-watch Season 3 of "Orange is the New Black" or should you work on your quadrant 2 activities?

The underlying value in this matrix is its simple ability to compare activities, which activities are really urgent, which are really important. Urgent activities require your immediate attention; important activities help you with your long-term goals.

THE EISENHOWER MATRIX

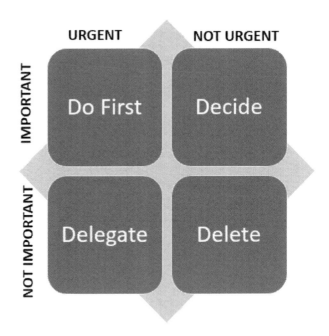

Organization Matters

Usually, college students aren't quite prepared to organize all the "stuff" in their lives as they transition to college. Dorm rooms can quickly get overrun with stuff like clothes, books, computers, mini-fridges, microwaves, television sets, and the other possessions of the college student's life.

Even if you're going to college locally and still living at home in the same room you've been in since you were a child, you still need to make room for the new trappings of college life. Try a few of these organization tips.

You will need a few supplies to get you started. First, you will need colored file folders, a portable plastic file holder, some colored binders, a 3-hole punch, and a few small bins will get you started.

Designate one color for each class and store pending assignments in them as you work on them. Place these folders inside the plastic holder. Be sure to write on the tab which class each folder is for to ease identification. You can also use the file folder approach to store important papers and receipts.

The colored binders are used for each class to store all the papers you receive in that class. As we talked about earlier, you will get a syllabus – put this in the front. Then, whenever you get a handout from your professor, place it in the binder. Use section dividers to label what information corresponds with which section. You should also keep completed assignments in this binder for easy referral, and in case your instructor "loses" one of your grades – then you can prove you did the work! It does happen, especially when your professor is handling hundreds of student assignments at any given time. Also, a professor may easily overwrite or enter a grade in the system wrong. Having an organized method to keep your assignments will make your life much easier when you sit down with your professor to review the mistake. You would be shocked to learn the number of times a student reaches out to me the last few weeks of the semester and asks for a copy of their initial assignment outlines, so they can get back to work on the project they were supposed to be working on all semester. Don't do this; it won't end well.

Keep on hand an ample supply of pens and #2 pencils, and use the bins for small items you accumulate like paper clips, push pins for a bulletin board, stapler, etc. It's a good idea to keep extra supplies like printer paper, and printer cartridges – just in case!

Now that you have the tools let's make sure you stay organized. Assignments can disappear in a pile of paper. Textbooks can get lost within a mound of laundry. A cluttered dorm room creates stress! Disorganization is all around us and happens practically everywhere, even in the most scholarly of places, like a college campus. But, there is an easy solution.

The rule with paper is very simple. There are only three things you can do with paper:

1. Act on it
2. File it
3. Toss it

For example, if you get a piece of mail, open it. Don't create a huge clutter problem by letting unopened mail pile up. You must decide what to do with your opened mail. If it is a catalog or a piece of junk mail and you know that you are not going to use, toss it. If it is a bill, pay it or mail it, or file it in a "bills due" folder. If you receive a memo or note, after reading it, toss it or file it away. If you get a paper returned, file it away. If you don't, the clutter and stress will build.

Another important place to de-clutter is your computer. If you can keep your files under control, you won't be looking in 20 different folders in "My Documents" for that English paper you wrote last week. Here are some suggestions to get rid of computer clutter.

• Deleting or archiving any e-mail you read will keep your inbox clean.

- Create a filing system- if you cannot reply right away, or need to save an e-mail, place in a folder made for that category. (Needs Reply, or Archives)

- Watch your "sent mail" folder. Delete or archive things from that as well.

- Add to your address book often. Many times, people will keep an e-mail in their inbox so that they have the address for the future. Instead of that, save the address. You'll know where to find it later.

- Utilize spam filters on your e-mail account to limit inbox distractions. Just don't forget to check your junk and spam mail folder for things that slipped through.

- Setting up folders by semester will keep your "My Documents" folder easier to navigate, as well as allow for quick reference.

- Move files to Dropbox or another backup device as a standard course of business. You don't want to lose any work and routinely backup your work in case of failure can save you untold time and stress.

Like any other skill, organization is a skill that can be learned. The most difficult part is breaking your lifelong bad habits. The key to getting better organized is to start with one small step and then take additional small steps one after the other. You may find that what you've put off for days takes only a few minutes to do. And once you see the benefits in one part of your life, you'll be motivated to expand this practice.

All the time management and organization tips in the world can only help if you put them to use. Putting things off can be the biggest mistake most college students make.

I'll Stop Procrastinating Today, Well Maybe Not Today!

Procrastination is a goal buster, wait it's more than that, it's a life buster. You might be thinking, isn't that a bit dramatic Professor Stemmle? I have always procrastinated, and I have gotten along just fine! I am here to tell you, what got you here, won't get you where you want to go. You must raise your game! And if you only change one bad habit make it to STOP procrastinating!

It's easy to put things off until later, especially when you dread the task such as writing a term paper. But in college, this is a real problem. If you put off your assignments or studying for tests, you are only hurting yourself. Procrastinating leads to stress and anxiety not to mention poor performance. You CAN stop procrastination from affecting your schoolwork.

Often students suffer from procrastination and find it difficult to get started working on their assignments. Most of the time, not starting seems to be related to a feeling of stress, fear or simply a feeling of being overwhelmed with the whole process. Aim to subdivide tasks into small steps and convince yourself that to get started all you need is five minutes working on the task. Often, the five minutes is all you'll need to get into the swing of things, and you can continue productively. I call this trick "The Five-Minute Hack."

Sometimes I hear students say they don't feel motivated to start their assignments; they are waiting for inspiration or a changing mood. I got news for you… people who wait on the mood to strike or motivation to hit them will find themselves doing everything last minute. Mood and Motivation aren't prerequisites to action…**it is a result of it!**

Try working for a short time and see if you can "get into it." If your motivation problem seems more substantial, it might help to realize that when you aren't motivated to do school work, you aren't out of motivation… **you are just motivated to do something else.**

Make every effort to develop the discipline you need to follow your plan. Your planner should always be handy, and you should refer to it often. Once you make your schedule, follow it. If you need help staying on task, work with a roommate or friend to motivate each other and hold each other accountable. Remind yourself you are focused on your long-term goals, and once you complete your work, you are one step closer to achieving those goals. And remember, by sticking to your plan, you will have more time for yourself.

If you are struggling to stick to your plan, try this tip. Make two activity lists: "Things I Like to Do" and "Things I Have to Do." Mix up activities from both lists and work on each activity for a short period. Alternating between fun and work helps to maintain motivation and interest. All work and no fun is another schedule buster. You don't have to be working ALL the time, but you do have to complete what is required to stay on plan.

Sometimes, you're going to feel overwhelmed with large projects or assignments. Remind yourself that this is a normal reaction. When you feel like this, it's easier to put things off because you don't know exactly where to start and have a difficult time envisioning the completed task. Divide these major assignments into smaller parts and work on one part at a time. Then put them together into the whole project and feel the satisfaction of a job well done!

You might have every intention of doing things promptly, but time can move swiftly. There are only 24 hours in a day, and some people are just over aggressive with their planning. Make sure your schedule is realistic, and you aren't involved in too many activities scheduled close together. If you spread yourself too thinly, none of your projects will get the attention they deserve.

Reward yourself when you complete tasks on time. Make the reward appropriate for the difficulty and boredom of the task. Utilizing rewards will help you stay on task and provide fuel for action.

Remember that you're not alone. Some studies report that up to 95% of college students experience procrastination as a real problem. Many students do most of the work in marathon sessions near academic deadlines and fail to make appropriate use of time management skills, tools, and study aids I recommend. Doing this leads to more stress in your already stressful life. Why add to your stress?

At this point, you are probably wondering why people procrastinate on tasks related to goals they want to achieve? Procrastination often emerges as a means of distancing oneself from stressful activities. People allocate more time to a task they judge as easy or fun than to tasks they judge as difficult or boring. Dealing with the underlying stressful aspects of the activities can assist in reducing the extent of procrastination. We'll address the problem of stress management a little later.

Pro Tip - If the volume of work on your to-do list overwhelms you, you might benefit from making a "one-item list." Re-write the top item from your list at the top of a blank page and work the task to completion, then take the next item on your list and place that on a blank sheet, repeat the process until you complete everything on your original list.

Some people must overcome procrastination gradually. Almost no one has trouble studying the night before a big exam. But without the pressure of an exam, many students find it easy to avoid studying. If you need the motivation of the looming deadline, remember to implement the five-minute hack.

The key is to learn the habit of getting started on a task early, i.e., the procrastinator needs to learn to initiate studying and preparing for papers and exams well in advance. Practice starting to study several times every day. As with exercising, getting started and making it a routine are the secrets to success. Other valuable suggestions include:

- Recognize self-defeating problems such as; fear and anxiety, difficulty concentrating, poor time management, indecisiveness, and perfectionism.

- Keep your goals in mind and identify your strengths and weaknesses, values and priorities.

- Compare your actions with the values you feel you have. Are your values consistent with your actions?

- Discipline yourself to use time wisely.

- A study session that utilizes small blocks of time with frequent breaks is more effective than studying in long uninterrupted marathon sessions. For example, you will accomplish more if you study/work in sixty-minute blocks and take frequent ten-minute breaks in between, than if you study/work for two to three hours straight, with no breaks.

- Reward yourself after you complete a successful week.

- Motivate yourself to study. Focus on success, not on failure. Try to study in small groups. Break large assignments into smaller tasks. Keep a reminder schedule and checklist.

- Set realistic goals.

- Modify your environment: Eliminate or minimize noise/distraction. Ensure adequate lighting. Have the necessary equipment at hand. Don't waste time going back and forth to get things. Don't get too comfortable when studying. A desk and a straight-backed chair are usually best (a bed is no place to study). Be neat! Take a few minutes to straighten your desk.

- Decide when you have had enough, and it's time for a change.

- Think about the activities that you use to procrastinate (email, TV, etc.) and set clear time limits on them.

- Set clear goals for each day (e.g., start CHEM problem set, do ENGL reading, finish MRKT chapter reading) and stick to them. Once complete, you are free to do whatever you like.

- Remember that serious academic stress usually follows procrastination.

- Recall the stress and loss of energy you felt the last time you had to stay up all night to write a paper or study for an exam. Remembering your feelings of anxiety can serve as an effective motivator to help you get started on time now.

- Know that overcoming procrastination is sometimes easier if you talk out strategies for change with someone else.

The Pomodoro Technique

Getting started is often the hardest part of any assignment, task, or project. The thought of sitting down in front of your computer for a few hours straight can cause you enough anxiety to want to head to the dentist instead. If that sounds like you have no fear, I have a solution for you. Enter the Pomodoro technique. A *Pomodoro* is simply the interval of time spent working.

The Pomodoro technique was originally designed as a time management technique, but in recent years it has been slightly modified to become an effective way to overcome procrastination.

The key to the success of this technique is that it only requires you to focus for 20-minutes at a time. After 20-minutes you get to take a 5-minute break. When your brain knows you will be able to reconnect to your social media, text a friend, or catch up on your email, it makes it much easier for you to engage and get started. And once started, you will build momentum, and you will be quite surprised just how much you will achieve.

To make this technique effective, it is important you are highly focused, you need to shut off your smartphone, shut off alerts on your other devices, and remove any other distractions. You need quiet, so if you have distractions that cannot be turned off, consider wearing noise reduction headphones or heading to the campus library.

In using the Pomodoro technique, you start by deciding what the first important task is for the day (utilize the Eisenhower Matrix). Then you set a timer for 20 minutes and focus 100% on that task.

When the timer chimes, reset it for 5-minutes, get up and do some deep breathing, stretch out your body, jump on social media, whatever you want to do for 5 minutes.

Next set the timer and jump back in for another 20-minutes and then repeat the 5- minute break. These 20- minute sprints are called a Pomodoro.

After doing four Pomodoro you have a completed set, now take a 20-minute break. Make sure you put a check mark on a piece of paper or notecard after each 20-minute Pomodoro, as it is quite easy to lose track of how many Pomodoro's you have completed.

As you get into the swing of things, feel free to adjust your Pomodoro's to 25-minutes, 30-minutes, or even 2-hours. I personally find a 2-hour Pomodoro with a 30-minutes break highly effective when I am writing books. When grading papers, I use the 20/5 approach outlined here. The point I want to make is that this technique is easily modified, play with the Pomodoro's to find what works best for you.

Why Procrastination Is a College Students Nightmare

Good ideas take time.   Whether you are working on a small assignment or a large paper, good ideas take time to develop and come together in a well-thought-out cohesive fashion. Most written assignments in college will require you to select a topic, then spend time developing your thoughts around your ideas, revising your thoughts, and finally fine-tuning and polishing things up.   If you procrastinate and wait until the last minute, you won't have time to properly go through an intellectual process required to ensure a fully reflective and developed piece of work. This approach also applies to essay questions on tests and exams. You will want to allow time to reflect on the question, rather than throwing out the first idea that pops into your head.

You will likely run out of time.   When it comes to strict deadlines-which is just about always in your college classes-you run the risk of missing the due date if you keep putting off your work until tomorrow. And the reality is that most professors will not give you an extension except in very special circumstances. It is not that they are trying to be mean, but once they make one exception, they will have to make hundreds. If your professor accepts late assignments, a grade penalty-often as much as one-third to one-half a grade a day will apply. Just don't take the risk.

You might be being overly dramatic. One of the key reasons we all procrastinate is to avoid the pain associated with actually doing the task at hand. In my experience, students overestimate the pain they'll feel while completing their assignments. It's quite understandable when faced with a 15-page paper, a 25-question problem set, or 50 pages of reading, you naturally feel the task is enormous and overwhelming, and the simple thought of starting makes your stomach sick. The reality is, if you just get started on a small piece and then another small piece, then another manageable piece, etc., you will see the assignment coming together, and your fear will disappear as you build on the positive momentum you have created.

The task is probably not as hard as you think. The reality is that thousands of students just like you have completed the task at hand. It's often hard to determine at the start of an assignment just how much time it'll take you to complete the assignment-especially if the topic is unfamiliar or covers a diverse area of topics. Just get started, and you will likely find that things are not as bad as you have built them up to be.

You lose your chance for help. Many students will want to enlist the help of the professor or a TA. But their time is limited, and many professors only maintain office hours a few hours a week on specific days only, and not every TA is timely when it comes to getting back to students. With the majority of students waiting to the last minute, a classic supply vs. demand problem is created, especially if the assignment is challenging, and 75% of the students have figured out they are stuck three days before the assignment is due. By starting your assignments early, you won't lose the chance to consult with the professor or TA in case you have questions. Even if you get answers to your questions at the last minute, you will not have time to implement your professor or TA suggestions, which will destroy your grade. Your Professor or TA will hate taking their time and providing feedback and suggestions to see you completely ignore their advice.

Contrary to what you might believe. You won't work better under time constraints. If you put off your work until the last minute, your work will be hurried and will demonstrate the shortcuts you took due to the time pressure. This experience will likely create stress, anxiety and even guilt for having put off the work once again. This behavior will take its toll on your sleep, energy, and mental well-being, it simply is not the best combination for your health or GPA.

Your work will look incomplete. One of the main differences between fair, good and excellent work is that excellent work has gone through a natural cycle of thoughts, drafts, and revisions. The paper will flow naturally and follow a well thought out logical sequence. When the clock is ticking, and your deadline is rapidly approaching, you will skip steps in the cycle and hand in an assignment that doesn't flow properly or hit on all the key ideas or concepts. Like a bad movie, the professor will easily notice the lack of effort that went into your work.

You place yourself at a relative disadvantage. While you're busy being busy, putting off your work for another time, some of your fellow students are getting down to business and getting started on their assignments. These students are likely going to raise the bar for everyone and increase the gap between excellent work, good work, and average work. Many professors will fit their grade curves to a somewhat normal distribution or even limit the percentage of students receiving an A. Most universities expect the grades in a class section to follow a somewhat normal distribution or average grade target ensuring a class is neither too difficult or too easy. The university won't talk about this in their orientations or course program guides, but rest assured behind those pillars of knowledge and opportunity, proper course curve fitting is being discussed and expected.

The task is the task. Some students think that somehow the task is going to get easier if they wait a little longer. If they give it a little more time, some miracle or inspiration will strike that will change the course of the assignment forever. Of course, this isn't going to happen; the assignment is the assignment once your professor assigned it. Get over it, and in the words of Nike, Just Do It!

Life happens. Anytime you have an assignment that covers some period or involves some research or builds upon lessons there is an increased likelihood that something distracting and unexpected will arise, thus stopping or greatly slowing down your ability to complete your work. You could catch the bug spreading around campus at the speed of a viral YouTube video, you could get food poisoning from the campus cafeteria, another professor could spring an assignment on you that requires unscheduled time, or some work or family emergency could pop up. Whatever the event, you can count on life getting in the way, and if you have properly planned and allowed some room in your schedule for these unplanned events, you will be able to deal with things and not tank your GPA.

Balancing class loads, assignments, work, and of course fun, can lead to a great deal of stress for the average college student. It's important to realize that this feeling is normal, and you are going to feel stressed with so much going on in your life. You can easily start to feel like your life is spiraling out of control, but you're not alone, and your fellow students are feeling somewhat the same way. Consider the following:

- 85% of college students reported they had felt overwhelmed by everything they had to do at some point in the past year.

- 42% of college students stated anxiety as the top concern.

- 30% of college students reported that stress had negatively affected their academic performance.

- 25% of college students reported they were taking psychotropic medication.

In the next chapter, we'll explore stress, what causes it, and how to lessen it.

College Life is Full of Excitement and Stress

"The only difference between stress and excitement is your attitude about it" — *unknown*

College Life is a Big Transition

College life is a big transition, and you can expect to face new anxieties as well. College can be the best of times and the worst of times. Meeting new people, learning new things, and being on your own are the things that shoot to the top of most student's lists. Falling behind in class, pulling "all-nighters" and preparing for exams are some of the negative experiences that shoot to the top of the list as well.

Sometimes it is those best of times experiences that lead to the worst of times experiences. Students who spend too much time focused on meeting new people and "socializing" find themselves missing class, falling behind on assignments, and "bombing" that critical exam.

Unfortunately, stress is a common and natural condition of our human existence. It arises through our daily efforts to achieve goals, relate with others, and adjust to the demands of living in this rapidly changing world.

We often view stress as a negative component in our lives and spend time trying to reduce or eliminate it. We forget that there can be a great deal of growth from learning how to deal with stressful situations.

Stress can make your heart race; increase your rate of breathing, and you may even start to break out in sweats. Most of us view stress as bad, but new research proposes that stress may only be bad for you if you believe stress is bad for you. Psychologist Kelly McGonigal recommends we see stress as a positive and promotes a mechanism for stress reduction: reaching out to others.

Let's look at a ground-breaking study that made many people rethink their outlook on stress. This study tracked 30,000 adults in the United States for eight years, and they asked people two key questions. First, "How much stress have you experienced in the last year?" Second, "Do you believe that stress is harmful to your health?" They tracked these participants and then used public death records to find out who died.

Let's start with the bad news first. People who reported that they had experienced a lot of stress in the previous year had a 43 percent increased risk of dying. But the game-changing information from the research was that the 43 percent increased risk of dying was only true for the people who also believed that stress was harmful to their health.

Amazingly, people who had experienced a lot of stress in the study, but did not view stress as a harmful influence on their health were no more likely to die. In fact, these people had the lowest risk of dying of anyone in the study, including the people who had reported relatively little stress.

Over the eight years of the study where the researchers were tracking deaths, 182,000 Americans died prematurely, not from stress itself, but from the belief that stress is bad for your health. Based on these estimates, that would make believing stress is bad for you the 15th largest cause of death in the United States.

What would happen if we believed that stress is not bad for us and that instead stress is just a natural response indicating that your body is becoming energized, your body is creating a physical state that is simply preparing you to meet the challenge ahead? The idea that stress could be good for us is what researchers wanted to research. Researchers at Harvard Universities told participants in a study that stress was good for them that stress was the bodies way of preparing you for a challenge ahead. Before exposing participants to the stress experiments, they went through the social stress test training. Participants were trained to understand that their stress response was not harmful but was in fact quite helpful. Researchers explained that their pounding heart is the bodies way of preparing you for action. If you're breathing faster, it's not a problem; it's your bodies way of getting more oxygen to your brain. The results of the study showed that participants who learned to view the stress response as helpful for their performance were less stressed out, less anxious, more confident. The fascinating finding was that participants physical stress responses changed.

In a typical stress response, your heart rate goes up, and your blood vessels constrict. It's not healthy to be in these state over long periods of time. But in the study, when participants viewed their stress response as helpful, their blood vessels stayed relaxed. Their heart was still pounding, but they had a much healthier cardiovascular profile. It looked a lot like what happens when we experience moments of joy. This biological change could be the difference between a stress-induced heart attack at age 60 and living well into your 90s. These studies are showing us that it is not the stress, but how you think about stress that makes all the difference.

I want to tell you about one more study, a study that could also save lives. This study tracked some 1,000 adults in the United States, who ranged in age from 34 to 93. In this study, they began by asking, "How much stress have you experienced in the last year?" They followed that by also asking, "How much time have you spent helping out friends, neighbors, people in your community?" And then they used public records for the next five years to find out who had died.

For every major stressful life experience that occurred, like financial troubles or a family crisis, people had an increased risk of dying by about 30 percent. But once again, this wasn't true for everyone. It turns out that people who had spent time caring for others showed absolutely no stress-related increase in dying. It seems that caring created a resilience to stress.

These studies show us that the harmful effects of stress on your health are not inevitable. It turns out, that how you think about stress, and how you act in stressful situations transforms your experience of stress. When you choose to view your stress response as helpful, you create a positive biological state, one that mirrors joyfulness or courage. And when you choose to connect and serve others while you are under stress, you can create a state of resilience.

Now I am not recommending you ask for more stressful experiences in your life, but the science should give you a whole new appreciation for stress. When we recognize stress as a positive, you're not just getting better at managing stress; you're making a pretty important statement. You're saying that you trust yourself to handle the challenges that life throws at you. You remember you're not alone, that others can still benefit from your help and that you understand that you don't have to face these challenges alone.

Our goal shouldn't be to eliminate stress, which in reality would be impossible, but to learn how to recognize our typical reactions to stress and then try to reframe our beliefs and responses about stress accordingly.

College is a particularly stressful time for most of us with the pressures of examinations, large amounts of reading, research papers, competition for grades, financial expenses, social pressures, and decisions about our futures. You can learn to effectively deal with stress rather than become discouraged and immobilized by it.

Each of us functions best at our unique stress level. When stress increases beyond that level, the effectiveness of our performance begins to drop. When we pass our peak of effectiveness, we usually experience symptoms like forgetfulness, dulled senses, poor concentration, headaches, stomach pains, restlessness, irritability, and anxiety. These symptoms are our bodies way of alerting us to take steps to reduce our stress, so our effectiveness and health can return to normal ranges.

Some people have a "racehorse" lifestyle and seem to thrive on intense activity while others prefer a "turtle" lifestyle and function best when their activity level is not intense. Trying to adopt a "turtle" lifestyle when we prefer a "racehorse" lifestyle, or vice-a-versa, can be stressful.

Your body's alert system functions much like a thermostat in your dorm room. Your thermostat's job is to keep your room on the temperature you set. If the temperature varies a degree or two in one direction or the other, you likely will not even notice the temperature change. Looking at the thermostat, you can see the temperature has changed, but it has changed within a range of acceptability. If your roommate had opened your window last night to let in a breeze in and forgot to close it in the morning and the cool morning turned into a hot August day in Florida, your air conditioning unit would become stressed and would not be able to maintain the temperature in your room. The temperature would rise to an extremely uncomfortable temperature. Shutting the window would allow your air-conditioning unit to catch up and your dorm room will return to the temperature you programmed into your thermostat. Leave the window open too long, with temperatures outside too hot, your air conditioning unit will be required to work too hard and can freeze up and stop working altogether.

We need to learn to trust our internal thermostats and adjust our schedules in a manner that is best for us. Never compare yourself to others who seem to function with a higher degree of stress in their lives than we do. Don't change your thermostat setting to match theirs. For example, we should register for the number of credit hours we think we can effectively handle even though our friends may register for more or fewer hours. Also, we should get the number of hours of sleep we need even though our roommates may function on fewer or more hours.

Here are several ideas that will help you reduce stress while in college.

First, and foremost, you need to make sure you are getting enough sleep. Most experts recommend 7-8 hours' sleep per night. Unfortunately, the average college student sleeps significantly less than then the recommended sleep amounts. Some student health surveys indicate that most college students sleep less than 6 hours and many less than 4 hours per night. And, you know you can't "pay it back." If you average 4-6 hours during the week, you can't sleep 12 on Saturday and catch up. In fact, if you sleep more than 8 hours you will likely feel more tired.

Drink plenty of water. Drinking water can increase your cognitive function. Your brain utilizes a significant amount of oxygen to function at an optimum level. Drinking plenty of water helps ensure that your brain gets all the oxygen it needs.

Drinking eight to ten cups of water per day can improve your levels of cognitive performance by as much as 30%!

Drinking plenty of water also helps support healthy nerve function. Proper hydration ensures your body's electrolyte levels remain high enough to allow your nerves to relay messages to and from the brain efficiently.

Another important stress management health tip is to ensure you eat regularly. Many college students skip breakfast, or lunch, sometimes going all day without eating. When you deprive your body of regular energy, it makes up for it by lowering your metabolism, or energy level. In other words, skipping meals does not help you lose weight or stay awake. In fact, it has the reverse effect.

The "quality" of food you eat is just as important as ensuring you eat regularly. Snack foods (chips, candy, fast foods, etc.) aren't the healthiest, and you should consume them in moderation. Highly salted foods can cause excess water retention and eventually lead to high blood pressure. Foods high in sugar can cause low blood sugar, or hypoglycemia; which can cause dizziness, tiredness, and fatigue. Instead, eat well-balanced meals, and nutritious snacks, such as fruit, protein bars, and nuts.

Regular exercise is a necessary part of any stress reduction program. Daily physical activity is essential in helping you stay focused, sharp, and performing at your best. Daily exercise breaks during mid-terms and finals week are a must, even if you take a short walk around campus to get away from your study area for a few minutes.

Alcohol and caffeine are the most widely used and abused substances by college students. Alcohol use certainly does not contribute to your ability to study and retain information.

If you are going to drink alcohol (and you are of legal age), do so in moderation. Drink only moderate amounts. Make sure you have a non-drinking designated driver if you are going to be driving. And, curtail your alcohol use a few days before major exams or projects. There's no better recipe for failure than a hangover and a calculus final to turn you into a college drop out.

Caffeine is widely used, especially around exam time. A few cups of coffee and pulling an "all-nighter" is still a fact of life at most colleges. But excess amounts of caffeine can lead to nervousness and forgetfulness.

Remember to take time for yourself. Play a video game, watch a movie, talk with friends. If you're feeling overwhelmed and stressed out, sometimes all you need is time away to relax and re-group.

Attitude is Everything!

"Attitude is everything." The way you think about things can make all the difference in how you react to events. Life is 20 percent what happens to you and 80 percent how you respond to what has happened to you. Have you ever noticed how the same situation could stress one person out, while it might not affect another person at all? The way each thinks about the situation drives their responses. Changing the way you think (a.k.a. cognitive restructuring) can help you manage stressors in your life. Here's how.

Each time something happens in our lives, the information about that event enters our brain. Our brain then interprets it; we form beliefs about what the event means to us, why it happened or how it is going to affect us. While we can't always control the events that happen, we can control what we think about the event, which in turn shapes our feelings about what we have experienced.

Self-talk is an ongoing internal dialogue we each have. Often this conversation is overly critical, irrational and destructive. To reduce stress, instead of being your own worst critic, be positive and kind to yourself.

Think about a stressful situation you experienced recently. Come up with both negative/irrational and productive/rational self-talk for the situation.

Example 1:

Situation: I have a very important paper due in two days that is worth twenty percent of my grade.

Irrational self-talk: I'll never get it done. Why did I take this stupid class in the first place?

Rational self-talk: I've worked well under pressure in the past. I know I can do it again!

Example 2:

Situation: I came home to discover my roommate left the place a complete mess.

Irrational self-talk: My roommate is always disrespectful to me. Why can't my roommate think about anyone but herself?

Rational self-talk: I know my roommate has a lot going on. She would have cleaned up if she had time.

Remember that you decide which self-talk will guide you. Try to monitor your self-talk and replace negative messages with constructive, positive, rational ones.

Try These Relaxation Techniques

There are also some relaxation techniques that can help you manage stress and also improve your concentration, productivity, and overall well-being.

Meditation

Mention the word meditation, and the images of some new age yogi quickly come to mind for many, but nothing could be further from the truth. Meditation and brain research have been rolling in steadily for some years now, with new studies coming out just about every week to illustrate some new benefit of meditation.

Did you know many famous and successful people credit meditation for their ability to gain focus, reduces stress, and energize themselves? Arnold Schwarzenegger, Steve Jobs, Oprah Winfrey, Jerry Seinfeld, Lady Gaga, Russell Simmons, Ellen DeGeneres, Cameron Diaz, Clint Eastwood, Katy Perry, and many more all practice meditation.

For those of you not swayed by the rich and famous, but driven by hard facts and science, this is for you. Forbes magazine reported that a team at Harvard found that mindfulness meditation can actually change the structure of the brain: Eight weeks of Mindfulness-Based Stress Reduction (MBSR) was found to increase cortical thickness in the hippocampus, which governs learning and memory, and in certain areas of the brain that play roles in emotion regulation and self-referential processing. There were also *decreases* in brain cell volume in the amygdala, which is responsible for fear, anxiety, and stress – and these changes matched the participants' self-reports of their stress levels, indicating that meditation not only changes the brain, but it changes our subjective perception and feelings as well. In fact, a follow-up study found that after meditation training, changes in brain areas linked to mood and arousal also linked to improvements in how participants said they felt — i.e., their psychological well-being.

So, what is meditation? Although, there are many types of meditation, at its core, meditation is about reaching a level of peace and silence effortlessly. As a result, you feel calm and refreshed. I recommend Transcendental Meditation or simply TM.

Initially, when you're first starting out, you will need a quiet environment. As you get more proficient at meditating, you will be able to do it anywhere despite the noise and distractions. However, when you're first starting out, silence is essential.

Assume a comfortable sitting posture. You could sit on a chair, bed or floor. The key point to note is that transcendental posture is a seated position. You do not do transcendental meditation while lying down. The goal is to meditate and not to drift off to slumberland.

With most types of meditation, there is a need to concentrate. The need to concentrate usually stresses people out further because they often find their mind drifting off or a million different thoughts enter their head while they're trying to meditate. Drifting off is perfectly normal. Even experts face this problem. It takes a lot of practice to silence the mind.

With the TM technique, there is no need to concentrate or focus. Transcendental meditation is supposed to be natural and effortless.

Once you're in the seated position, you could place your hands on your lap or by your side. Next, you will chant a rudimentary sound that doesn't have any meaning. You do not want the sound you make to conjure any thoughts or images.

The sound you make could be an "aaaaahhh" or "ummmmmm." It doesn't matter what the sound is as long as it's comfortable for you. The simple sound you make is called a mantra or chant.

Imagine all your thoughts rotating around this chant. The chant is like a cone spiraling downwards. Initially, you may have thoughts popping up. Do not force them to disappear. There should not be an effort here. Stay focused on the chant as it leads you down the zone where there is little thought.

When your mind drifts, gently guide it back by focusing on your mantra. After some time, your thoughts will slow down gradually and diminish. It will happen on its own accord without forcing.

As you approach the "zone" where there is not much thought, you will notice that the tension in your body starts dissipating. Your heart rate will slow down, and you might experience a tingling sensation in your hands and feet. It's all perfectly normal.

Now that you're in the zone, you should try and remain in this zone for about 20 minutes. Any thoughts that form will usually dissolve into nothing. You are at rest, and you're doing it right. When returning thoughts start running amok, refocus on the mantra and return to the zone.

That pretty much sums it up. Aim to do this twice daily – Once in the morning and once later in the day or early evening. Here are a few quick tips.

1. Wear loose, comfortable clothing. Sit in a relaxing position.

2. Close your eyes and concentrate on a calming thought, word or object.

3. You may find that other thoughts pop into your mind. Don't worry, this is normal. Try not to dwell on them. Just keep focusing on your image or sound.

4. If you're having trouble, try repeating a word or sound over and over. (Some people find it helpful to play soothing music while meditating.

5. Gradually, you'll begin to feel more and more relaxed.

Progressive Muscle Relaxation

This technique can help you relax the major muscle groups in your body. And, it's easy to do. In this relaxation technique, you focus on slowly tensing and then relaxing each muscle group. Applying this technique will help you recognize the difference between muscle tension and relaxation. You will become more aware of physical sensations and learn to pay attention to your body. Tense your muscles for about five to ten seconds and then relax for 30 seconds, and repeat.

1. Wear loose, comfortable clothing. Sit in a favorite chair or lie down

2. Begin with your facial muscles. Frown hard for 5-10 seconds and then relax all your muscles.

3. Work other facial muscles by scrunching your face or raising your eyebrows for 5-10 seconds. Release. You should feel a noticeable difference between the tense and relaxed muscles.

4. Move to your jaw. Then, move on to other muscle groups – shoulders, arms, chest, legs, etc. – until you've tensed and relaxed individual muscle groups throughout your whole body.

Visualization

This technique uses your imagination, a great resource when it comes to reducing stress. In this relaxation technique, you form mental images to take a visual journey to a peaceful, calming place or situation. To relax using visualization, try to incorporate as many senses as you can, including smell, sight, sound, and touch. If you imagine relaxing at the ocean, for instance, think about the smell of salt water, the sound of crashing waves and the warmth of the sun on your body. You may want to close your eyes, sit in a quiet spot, loosen any tight clothing, and concentrate on your breathing. Aim to focus on the present and think positive thoughts.

1. Sit or lie down in a comfortable position.

2. Imagine a pleasant, peaceful scene, such as a lush forest or a sandy beach. Picture yourself in this setting.

3. Focus on the scene for a set amount of time (any amount of time you are comfortable with), then gradually return to the present.

Deep Breathing

One of the easiest ways to relieve tension is deep breathing. Follow these steps to get started.

1. Lie on your back with a pillow under your head. Bend your knees (or put a pillow under them) to relax your stomach.

2. Put one hand on your stomach, just below your rib cage.

3. Slowly breathe in through your nose. Your stomach should feel like it's contracting.

4. Exhale slowly through your mouth, emptying your lungs completely and letting your stomach expand.

5. Repeat several times until you feel calm and relaxed. Practice daily.

Is This My Problem?

A major source of stress is people's efforts to control events or other people over whom they have little or no power. When confronted with a stressful situation, ask yourself: is this my problem? If it isn't, leave it alone. If it is, can you resolve it now? Once you resolve the problem, leave it alone. Don't agonize over the decision and try to accept situations you cannot change.

There are many circumstances in life beyond your control, starting with the weather and ending with the behavior of others. Remind yourself that we live in an imperfect world. Know your limits. If a problem is beyond your control and you cannot make a change at the moment, don't fight the situation. Learn to accept what is, for now, until such time when you can change things.

"No one can make you feel inferior without your consent" - Eleanor Roosevelt

Many students find it helpful to remember three little words – Let It Go. If you can change something, then change it. If you can't, Let It Go. Once you put this thought process into practice, you'll be surprised at how much stress leaves your body. If we dwell on the past or on situations that we cannot change, stress is compounded and magnified. So, remind yourself, if you can't do anything about it, Let It Go!

Be mindful that excessive stress can lead to depression. Warning signs include:

- Sadness, anxiety, or "empty" feelings.

- Decreased energy, fatigue, being "slowed down."
- Loss of interest or pleasure in activities you usually enjoy.
- Sleep disturbances (insomnia, oversleeping, or waking much earlier than usual).
- Appetite and weight changes (either loss or gain).
- Feelings of hopelessness, guilt, and worthlessness.
- Thoughts of death or suicide, or suicide attempts.
- Difficulty concentrating, making decisions, or remembering.
- Irritability or excessive crying.
- Chronic aches and pains not explained by another physical condition.

If you find yourself experiencing any of the symptoms listed above for a prolonged period-of-time – seek help! Most campuses have resources available such as counseling to help stressed-out and depressed college students cope. Don't let yourself believe that "it's just the blues." Sometimes feeling down can spiral out of control. There are many medications and solutions available to treat depression and make the sun shine again!

FIND HELP

Most college and university campuses have mental health resources available for students.

ON-CAMPUS

- Visit your campus health or counseling center and ask about their counseling services.

- Call the psychology or behavioral health department and ask about counseling sessions with graduate students.

- Visit your school's chaplain, religious or spiritual leader.

- Confide in a friend, RA, professor or mentor. Ask him or her to go with you to seek professional help.

OFF-CAMPUS

- Visit your family physician, who may be able to treat you or refer you to a professional who specializes in the specific disorder.

- Confide in a parent or relative. Ask him or her to support your efforts in finding help.

- Search the ADAA "Find a Therapist" database for a mental health professional in your area.

- Find a local support group. Many counseling centers, hospitals, community centers, and places of worship run or host support groups.

Learn more about mental health and college students at:
www.adaa.org

 ANXIETY AND DEPRESSION ASSOCIATION OF AMERICA

1. 2015 National College Health Assessment
2. 2013 Association for University and College Counseling Center Directors Survey

Garbage or Gold, You Decide!

It is easy to create a habit out of seeing only the negative when you are highly stressed. Some people have spent their entire lives "turning gold into the garbage - the Midas touch in reverse." Don't be one of those people.

If someone says, "That's a nice outfit" the "garbage collector" wonders, "What do they mean." Your thoughts can become like a dark pair of sunglasses, allowing little light or happiness into your life. Please accept a challenge, one that sounds simple, but will be harder than you think. For the next three days, commit yourself to actively collecting (noticing) five "pieces of gold" from your environment? When the garbage thoughts enter your head, pause and ask where is the piece of gold?

Pieces of gold are positive thoughts or interactions. These may seem like small or trivial things but as these "pieces of gold" accumulate they can often provide a big lift to energy and spirits and help you begin to see things in a new, more balanced way – on the road to a less stressful life! You will start to train your brain to respond more positively and productively to events in your life.

Each day you should find twenty minutes of "alone time" to relax. Take a walk, write in a journal or meditate. Don't sweat the small stuff, ask yourself if the issue at hand is worth derailing you from your goals. If it isn't affecting your goal achievement, it is not worth burning any brain cells or stressing over it.

Talking to a person who you trust be they a friend, roommate, family member, professor, significant other or co-worker about issues of concern is helpful. We all need someone to listen.

A huge part of taking control of your stress is to prevent it before it happens in the first place. Good study habits are an important tool for reducing stress and for effective time management. You may have been studying your whole academic life, but in college, things are different. Effective study habits lead to a more positive college experience both in and out of class.

Effective Study Habits!

Many college students struggle to figure out the right amount of time to dedicate toward studying. As we mentioned before, cramming and pulling "all-nighters" is still a fact of life on most college campuses. These types of sessions increase stress levels and don't always lead to the best performances.

Learning how to study effectively can be the best way to manage your time and leave a little left over for some hobbies clubs, working out, sports a job, parties, and relaxation. Here are some tips to consider:

Identify your "Best Time" for Studying: Everyone has high and low periods of attention and concentration. Are you a "morning person" or a "night person"? Use your high energy times to study; use the down times for routines such as laundry and errands.

Study Difficult Subjects: Study difficult material when you are well rested as you will process information better and save time.

Use Distributed Learning and Practice: Study in shorter time blocks taking short breaks. Smaller blocks of study time will keep you from getting fatigued and "wasting time." This type of studying is efficient because while you are taking a break, the brain is still processing information.

Make Sure the Surroundings are Conducive to Studying: This will allow you to reduce distractions which can "waste time." There will be times in the residence halls or your apartment when you know there will be noise and commotion, have a backup study location or use that time for mindless tasks.

Make Room for Entertainment and Relaxation: College is more than studying. You need to have a social life, yet, you need to have a balance in your life.

Make Sure You Have Time to Sleep and Eat Properly: Sleep is often an activity (or lack of activity) that students use as their time management "bank." When they need a few extra hours for studying or socializing, they withdraw a few hours of sleep. Doing this makes the time they spend studying less effective because they will need a couple of hours of clock time to get an hour of actual productive time.

Notecards

Notecards are a gift from above for those classes that seem to revolve around definitions, dates, or memorizing equations. If you're really smart, while reading the class material, you will take the time to copy definitions or important facts onto a 3" x 5" index card. When you finish the chapter, you should have a little stack of compact information that will prove to be invaluable.

Don't try to copy everything down. Concentrate on the major points that you'll need to remember test time. The simple act of writing down the information will make your brain start to think about the new information and retain it easier.

When you look back over the cards, you might be surprised that you can remember some of what you just wrote down before your studying even begins. Keep making cards for the new material you read and get in class lecture. When test time comes, you won't have to waste your time going back through notes and books trying to sift the important information away from the filler. You've already assembled all the material you need to study, and in most cases, it will fit right into your pocket!

Sit down two or three days before an exam and go through your notecards. Try to reproduce all the definitions – either by saying them out loud or writing them down. Writing takes longer to do, but in most cases, you will remember them faster and retain them longer if you have to write them down, thus saving you time in the long run.

Once you learn the information on your card, put a tally mark in the corner. When you have three to five tally marks on a card (depending on how well you think you need to know the material), then you can be pretty certain you know your stuff. Soon the cards you know readily will be marked up with tally marks, and the ones that are tricky will be left. Study the tricky cards extra hard, and when all your notecards have tally marks, you're finished.

The night before the test arrives, your companions are sifting through notes, books, copies of slides, etc., but you calmly reach for your notecards and review stuff that you already knew two days ago. Maybe you've forgotten some, no problem. Review them a couple more times, slap down some more tally marks when you get them right, and again, you're finished.

And guess what? A few months down the line you're going to have a final. One of the most difficult things about studying for finals is that you have to gather all the information for the entire semester so that you can study it. Some people spend all week copying old notes, reviewing book material, etc., to get ready to study for exams.

But, if you've been making notecards and keeping them, you should have a convenient little pile of things you should know. You don't have to spend time sifting through an entire semester of information because you've been doing that already, one day at a time. You're ready to study.

Plus, you can always have your notecards with you , so you can take advantage of downtime – waiting in lines, waiting to see the doctor, waiting for your Starbucks. Maximizing downtime with notecards makes tedious studying much, much easier. Don't want to carry all those note cards around with you, take a few photos of your cards with your smartphone and study anytime you are on the go.

Reading your English textbook isn't the most interesting thing on your to-do list. We know that. There is an effective technique you can use while reading, though, that will help maximize what you get out of the material especially if your professor is using a text that highlights the learning objectives for each chapter. It may seem complicated at first, but once you get into the habit of doing it, many students notice a marketable change in how they study.

The technique is called SQ3R – survey, question, read, recite, review. It is a proven way to sharpen your study skills. Here's how it works:

Survey - get the best overall picture of what you're going to study before you study it in any detail. It's like looking at a road map before going on a trip. If you don't know the territory, studying a map is the best way to begin.

Question - ask questions for learning. The important things to learn are usually answers to questions. Questions should lead to an emphasis on the what, why, how, when, who and where of study content.

Ask yourself questions as you read or study. As you answer them, you will help to make sense of the material and remember it more easily because this process will make an impression on you. Those things that make impressions are more meaningful, and therefore more easily remembered. Don't be afraid to write your questions in the margins of textbooks, on lecture notes, or wherever it makes sense.

Read - Reading is NOT running your eyes over a textbook. When you read, read actively. Read to answer questions you have asked yourself or questions the instructor or author has asked. Always be alert to bold or italicized print. The authors intend that this material receive special emphasis. Also, when you read, be sure to read everything, including tables, graphs, and illustrations. Often, tables, graphs, and illustrations can convey an idea more powerfully than written text.

Recite - When you recite, you stop reading periodically to recall what you have read. Try to recall main headings, important ideas for concepts presented in bold or italicized type, and what graphs, charts, or illustrations indicate. Try to develop an overall concept of what you have read in your own words and thoughts. Try to connect things you have just read to things you already know. When you do this, the chances are you will remember much more of the lesson and be able to recall material for papers, essays and objective tests easier.

Review - A review is a survey of what you have covered. It is a review of what you are supposed to accomplish not what you are going to do. Rereading is an important part of the review process. Reread with the idea that you measure what you have gained from the process.

During the review, it's a good time to go over notes you have taken to help clarify points you may have missed or don't understand. The best time to review is when you have just finished studying something. Don't wait until just before an examination to begin the review process. Before an examination, do a final review. If you manage your time, the final review will serve as a "fine-tuning" of your knowledge of the material.

Learn to keep notes logically and legibly. Remember, if you can't read your writing a few days after taking notes, they are of little use. By all accounts, the best place to keep notes is in a loose-leaf notebook. Use dividers to separate the different classes you take. Make it a habit of using your notebook to record ALL your notes.

If you're caught without your notebook and need to take notes, always have a supply of loose-leaf paper or notecards with you. Insert your notepapers into the notebook as soon as you can. Be sure to buy a good notebook, as it will get a lot of wear and tear.

Many critics of the SQ3R method cite the extensive amount of time that is required to implement this study method. I tend to agree that SQ3R can be very time-consuming. Most students find this approach only worth their investment for their difficult and complex courses. The key is to understand that this approach may be valuable for you and that it is available for use when needed.

These are just a few of the many successful tips and strategies you can use to reduce stress and improve your GPA. I don't have enough time in this book to go over all the tools and strategies for college success, but for those of you wanting to learn more about how you can be successful in college, you can head over to a special website I have set up for the readers of this book www. IWantCollegeSuccess.com.

How to Get and Stay Motivated

"There will be obstacles. There will be doubters. There will be mistakes. But with hard work, there are no limits." — Michael Phelps

There are plenty of articles, books and blog posts on motivation that tell you how to become more motivated. Often, these resources just hit on the surface of motivation.

These ideas are useful to an extent, but they ultimately fall short. If you struggle with motivation and can't keep yourself focused on new tasks, then a tip or two isn't going to transform your ability to focus overnight.

And if you struggle to motivate yourself, how are you expected to keep up the changes that lead to greater motivation? It's something of a vicious circle don't you think?

If you want to see changes, then you need to look a little deeper. You need to focus on the actual neuroscience that underpins our ability to get and stay motivated. In this chapter, you'll learn exactly how motivation works on a biological level, and more importantly, you'll discover how you can manipulate that process to your ends.

Introducing the Salience Network

What we're interested in here is what neuroscientists and psychologists refer to as attentional control or executive attention, which describes the ability we have to direct our attention and hold it – the power we have over what we choose to focus on and what we choose to ignore.

How does all this science stuff work in your brain? It comes down to several frontal regions within the brain that control our ability to focus. Perhaps most notable in the process is the anterior cingulate cortex which lately has been the result of a fair amount of research.

It turns out; two separate networks or brain regions determine our brain's ability to concentrate: areas that work together to achieve the desired result. Specifically, these networks are known as the dorsal attention network which includes brain regions that run along the top of the brain (dorsal means "top" in biology – hence "dorsal fin") and the ventral attention network (which runs along the bottom).

Understanding these two different attention networks is key because they have different purposes that clue us in on how to get superior attention. The dorsal attention network is concerned with our intentional attention (a bit of a tongue twister). In other words, when you decide that you want to focus on your math book for a while, or you choose to check your smartphone, you are using the dorsal network.

When we find our attention reflexively directed beyond our control that is the ventral attention network doing its job. In other words, when you hear a loud bang and you turn to look at it; that is your ventral attention network at work.

But your ventral attention network can also be distracted by a range of other biological clues. If you are hungry for instance, then your ventral attention network will begin to direct your attention toward getting food, and if you are tired, then your ventral attention network will direct your attention toward rest.

So, if you're trying to get work done and things keep distracting your attention, then it is going to be hard for you to maintain your attention!

The next question we need to ask is how the brain knows what should get its attention. The answer comes down to, yet another neural network called the salience network. This network tells us what is important and what isn't, and it appears to connect closely to our ability to motivate ourselves.

In other words, those with the ability to tell their brain what is important will be able to stay focused on work, they'll be able to run longer distances, and they're able to stay intensely focused during competition. But what if you weren't born with a powerful salience network? What can you do to fix the situation?

Taking Back Control

The answer comes down to our evolutionary history. Every aspect of our psychology evolved the way it did to help us survive. Traits that proved conducive to our long-term survival would be passed on to our offspring and those that did not would eventually die out.

Thus, the job of this network is to alert us to things that are important for our survival –biological signals from the body and our brain's associations trigger these alerts. If you see a bear, then your salience network will identify this as important, it will trigger the ventral attention network, and this will direct your attention there.

The result will be that your parasympathetic nervous system kicks in and triggers a hormonal and neurochemical response: you'll produce adrenaline, dopamine, cortisol, and norepinephrine and these chemicals will raise the heart rate contract your muscles and narrow your attention to that one thing.

To a lesser extent, this happens if you're hungry, too hot, too cold, or if you are experiencing stress about something else whether that be your English class, an upcoming exam, a relationship or anything else.

The first thing you need to do then to improve your ability to focus and stay motivated is to ensure that you remove these distractions that can override your dorsal attention network. To achieve the correct environment you need to create a working environment that will be free from distractions, and that makes you as comfortable as possible. Any loud noise, any discomfort, any hunger or any lingering stress can potentially make it hard for you to maintain your focus.

One trick that you can use to encourage a more focused state of mind comes from WordPress creator Matt Mullenweg. He described to Tim Ferriss during a podcast interview, how he would listen to music he knew well on repeat. The music would play over and over again, and he would become immensely familiar with it. As a result, the brain would then start to phase that music out. In other words, it would become desensitized to it, just as you eventually stop hearing the ticking of the clock. If you are listening to that music through headphones, it will drown out other noise.

By repeating music you effectively create a kind of sensory deprivation. The only sound there is completely blocked out by the brain. You can achieve something similar by using white noise, and this is something that many people will use to focus while working. Similar to white noise are other innocuous sounds, such as the rain or background chatter. Rainymood.com and coffitivity.com are both sites that provide these kinds of looping sounds for you to block out your surroundings.

Another trick to help you stay focused while doing computer work is to use a widescreen monitor. Studies show that widescreen monitors can increase productivity by up to thirty percent. A 22-inch widescreen monitor has a productivity gain of about thirty percent over a 19-inch standard monitor. Productivity seems to peak with a 26-inch widescreen monitor, which further improves productivity by twenty percent over the 22-inch monitor.

One of the most important things you can do to maintain your focus is to try to remove all other stress from your mind. That means that you need to try and stop worrying about your GPA and even about the other work you have to do that day. If you are worried about those things, then your brain will keep being distracted away from what you need to do. So, try to learn to block out feelings of stress and anxiety and to focus on the task that is at hand. Blocking out distractions will take practice, but your brain is like any other muscle – the more you train it, the greater the control you will get over it.

Jedi Mind Tricks

But we need to go further than this if we're going take complete control over our motivation. Ideally, we need to ensure that our ventral and dorsal attention networks are aligned. How do we do this?

The answer lies in the reason that we are distracted in the first place. The reality is not just that we think other things are more important at the time, but also that we feel what we should be doing isn't important or is just plain boring. You consciously might know that you need to study, go to the gym or library, but you are not feeling it. That's your dorsal network doing its work.

But your body doesn't know that. To your body, this is an unstimulating activity that isn't serving any of your prime directives. One thing our brain needs is stimulation, and that corresponds with a neural activity that comes from doing something that seems biologically important. Stimulation is why we find it easy to focus on video games, social media accounts or YouTube – they simulate exciting, important events happening, all charged with emotion. Entering class notes into a Word document though? Not so much.

But our human intelligence comes from our ability to focus not just on what is biologically important right now but on what we need to be doing in the distant future. In other words, we can extrapolate, plan, and predict, and that ability has made us highly effective.

The ability to understand the ramification of our actions comes from our working memory, which is our ability to store information in our "mind's eye" as it were. We can focus on things that have happened, or things we think could happen, and this causes the brain to light up as though they are happening. The process we are experiencing is visualization – we're internalizing our experience to be able to manipulate the variables.

One way to give yourself more motivation is to learn to link the boring event or the thing you don't want to do, to the worthwhile and important goal that you hope to achieve.

In other words, you need to remind your brain why the task at hand is important. If you're typing out a spreadsheet, then visualize how this is going to eventually lead to you being wealthier, more successful in your career and less stressed tonight. Consider what will happen if you don't do it – you will be behind with your class work, and you won't be able to accomplish the goals you're aiming to achieve!

If you're struggling to motivate yourself to go to the gym, then imagine what your life will be like when you're in great shape. Seem worth it now?

Another tip is to make whatever you're doing more interesting and more fun, which makes it more salient to your brain. I always say that the best cure for writer's block, in particular, is to make the scene or the paragraph you're writing more interesting. If it's not interesting enough to write, then it likely won't be interesting to read!

If you're doing data entry for a lab project, then make it a little more rewarding by putting the TV on in the background on mute – as long as it isn't too distracting to prevent you from paying attention to what you're doing. Oh, and once you get into the flow – make sure that there is nothing there to break that concentration. Put your phone on silent.

Master Your Brain

"The mind is the limit. As long as the mind can envision the fact that you can do something, you can do it, as long as you believe 100 percent." —
Arnold Schwarzenegger

If you were to buy a car, a computer, a gaming console or even a new tech device, then in all likelihood it would come with an instruction manual of some sort so that you could find your way around its features and how you should use it.

The user manual is important because it allows you to get the very most from your new purchase and it allows you to avoid making mistakes that could damage it.

But unfortunately, the most important and most complex things in the world come with no such instruction manual. Take children; for example, any new parent will tell you just how dismayed they were when they realized that no one could tell them how to be an effective mother/father.

And then there's the big one, our brains. These are the most complex supercomputers in the entire world, and they are what create all of our subjective feelings, sensations, and experiences. And yet our brains come with no instructions and no guidance: we are left simply to try and figure them out on our own. So, the question then becomes: How can you master your brain?

Fortunately, neuroscientists and psychologists are uncovering more of the brain's secrets every single day. While there is still a huge amount left to learn, we know more than we ever did, and a lot of this information can be used practically to help us become happier, smarter and more effective versions of ourselves. Read on, and you will see how you can master your brain for complete and total self-mastery.

Neuroscience is a subject that can take decades to learn and even then, it will be necessary to specialize in a specific area – as I said, it's a complex piece of machinery. There is much more than can be explained here, but we can nevertheless give a brief overview to give you some important clues as to how the brain essentially works. So, what do we know?

First of all, the brain is made up of neurons. These neurons are cells that have long tendrils called axons and dendrites. These reach out to almost touch each other and that in turn means that they will be close enough for small signals to jump across the gap. In turn, creating a huge map made up of billions of neurons with incredibly intricate connections. This network is called the "connectome," and everyone's is slightly different. These individual differences are what give us our different skills and abilities and our different personalities.

These neurons are responsible for mapping every single experience that you have. Each neuron represents a sensation, a memory, an experience, a feeling or something else. Your vision maps to a huge array of neurons that represent what you see, and likewise, your memory is made up of lots of interlinked neurons that reflect your thoughts and ideas.

These neurons are grouped roughly into different regions throughout the brain based on their function. In the occipital lobe, for instance, we have all the neurons responsible for our vision. In the motor cortex, we have neurons that correspond with movements and sensations throughout our body. Our prefrontal cortex is where we handle things like planning and motivation. Our brain stem handles breathing. And our hippocampus stores many of our memories. The different regions of the brain explain why damage to one specific area of the brain can result in a loss of specific function, and this organization is so extreme that there have even been cases where a head trauma has led to a patient losing their memory in one area yet impacting no other areas.

Interactions between neurons occur through "action potentials." These are electrical impulses that occur once a neuron has received enough stimulation. That stimulation is normally the result of lots of nearby neurons firing enough to put it past a certain excitability threshold. When an action potential occurs, this can also result in the release of neurotransmitters. These are chemicals released from vesicles (sacs) that alter the way that neurons work– perhaps making them more or less likely to fire, or perhaps making the event seem more or less important/sad/happy/memorable.

Another factor that influences our differences is our balance of neurotransmitters and hormones. If you have lots of the feel-good neurotransmitter serotonin, then you will often be in a good mood, and you'll be relaxed. If you have lots of cortisol and glutamate, then you will be a more wired and panicked kind of person.

Neurotransmitters and Outside Influences

What's important to recognize here, is that those neurotransmitters are not just a result of what is happening in the brain but can also be a result of biological signals from our bodies. For example, if you have low blood sugar, then your brain produces more of the stress hormone cortisol. Our bodies evolutionary response is intended to make us seek out more food – but it is also the reason that we tend to feel anxious and angry when we haven't eaten for a while.

Conversely, serotonin can be released when we eat something and our blood sugar spikes. Serotonin is why we feel good when we've just eaten. That serotonin eventually converts to melatonin though, which is the sleep neurotransmitter, and which suppresses neural activity. Melatonin is why we will often feel tired and sleepy after a big meal.

Countless other things also influence our balance of brain chemicals. Bright light, for instance, can reduce the production of melatonin and increase the production of cortisol and nitric oxide to wake us up. Remember: there were no artificial lights in the wild, and so our brain could rely solely on this signal to know what time of day it was!

While there is much more to it than that, this very generally describes the form and function of the brain and how it gives rise to our individual experiences.

Brain Plasticity

Another aspect of the brain that is very important to familiarize yourself with is plasticity. Brain plasticity (also called neuroplasticity) is the brain's ability to adapt and grow.

For a long time, we believed the brain only formed new neurons and new connections during childhood, and after that point, no growth occurred. However, we now know that this process continues until we die and is a crucial aspect of the way our brain functions. It does slow down slightly in adults, but it is still what gives us the ability to learn, to change our minds and to acquire new skills.

94

Neural plasticity occurs through practice, repetition, and events that we believe to be very important. The saying among neuroscientists goes: "what fires together, wires together." In other words, if you experience something, a neuron will light up. If you experience that thing at the same time as another thing, two neurons might light up (or more likely, two groups of thousands of neurons).

If you keep re-experiencing those two things together, a connection between them will begin to form. Subsequently, that connection will become stronger through a process called myelination during which the dendrites and axons become insulated to conduct the flow of electricity better. Eventually, one neuron firing will cause the other neuron to fire. Neurons firing allow you to learn a complex series of movements when dancing, or how you can memorize words in a new language.

At this point, I am sure the question you are having is how you can productively use this information?

Controlling Neurotransmitters

One way to hack your brain for greater productivity, happiness or whatever else, is by influencing the production of neurotransmitters. We've learned that these influence our mood and our ability to learn, so changing the balance of these chemicals could certainly be very useful.

Neurotransmitter balance is why a lot of people are interested in the idea of nootropics. Nootropics are smart drugs, supplements, and medications that can influence the production of neurotransmitters so that we have more goal-oriented dopamine or less fear-inducing cortisol. Modafinil alters the production of orexin, which can completely change our sleep/wake cycle, so we feel more awake. Influencing balance is also what caffeine does, by removing the inhibitory neurotransmitter adenosine (or neutralizing it, to be more precise).

The problem with this strategy is that it fixes the brain into a specific, unnatural state and prevents you from being able to easily switch modes. No one brain state is superior to all others – for example, creativity requires relaxation, not stimulation.

Worse, the brain can adapt to those changes by creating more or less receptor sites (the points where the neurotransmitters work) to make us more or less sensitive to the neurotransmitters in question. An overdependence on an unnatural brain state can eventually lead to addiction.

Some neurotransmitters work better by focusing more on neuroplasticity, or more on energy production, but for the most part, this is not the solution.

What is a much more useful solution is for us to look at those factors that naturally influence neurotransmitter release and balance. If you want to hack any system, you need to understand what the inputs are.

So, we know that bright light can increase energy and make us less sleepy, so why not consider investing in a daylight lamp which is designed to combat SAD (Seasonal Affective Disorder) by simulating the sun's rays? We know that cold likewise can increase focus, while heat can help us to feel more relaxed and happier. We know that the sun and that exercise can boost our mood through the production of serotonin.

We also know that our brain is subject to certain natural cycles, those relating to sleep and hunger for instance. By timing our productivity around those things, we can work more effectively and free from distraction.

And if you find yourself feeling very stressed or depressed, then it might pay to consider some of the biological factors that may be causing that. Perhaps you're hungry? Or perhaps you're a little ill, and the pro-inflammatory cytokines are causing brain fog? Once you know the problem is transient and biological, it can be much easier just to let it pass.

Controlling Your Brain

It is critical that you learn to create the moods and the feelings that you need by changing the way you think and use your brain.

The thing that makes humans unique is our ability to visualize – to internalize events and to imagine future scenarios or possibilities. Visualization is our working memory at play, and it is what enables us to think of long-term goals and to invent new ideas. And if you believe in the theory of embodied cognition, then you might find that this is what we use to understand plain English (look it up – it's fascinating!).

When we visualize or imagine, we do so by lighting up the same neurons in the brain as though the event were happening. Neurologically, we find doing something and imagining doing something almost indistinguishable.

Given this neurological response means that you can use visualization to practice things and develop skills – you can trigger brain plasticity just as though you were practicing the event! Not only that, but you can also use this as a way to trigger the appropriate neurotransmitters to put yourself in the correct state of mind.

Ultimately, this will lead to the ability to control your own emotions – to trigger the best possible mental state for the task at hand. It requires training of your visualization skills and the awareness to use those skills to ease your anxiety and to motivate yourself to focus and to become more alert as necessary. Managing your emotions is the neuroscience that underlies psychological approaches such as cognitive behavioral therapy and philosophies such as stoicism.

It is also important to avoid bad habits – even bad habits in our thoughts – as ruminating and indulging strengthens connections that make those habits harder and harder to break.

There's a lot more to making the most from your brain, but I hope this basic primer has given you a better understanding of the brain.

Energy and Time Management

"Energy and persistence conquer all things." —
Benjamin Franklin

Your energy level and motivation are key attributes to successful time management. Just knowing what to do is not enough. Knowledge without proper action will not drive positive results. As Mark Twain was fond of saying "The man who does not read good books has no advantage over the man who can't read them."

Your energy, just like your time, is finite. Only it exists in somewhat smaller quantities meaning that it's all too easy to run out and end up completely exhausted. And that's when we start to use our time poorly and not get much done. Many will argue that you have plenty of time. Most of us do have a lot of time; otherwise, how did you manage to stream that entire season of your favorite Netflix or Amazon series? How did you find time for that latest's live stream, or how did you spend two hours today on your social media feeds? And even the busiest of us usually find time for sleep!

The point here is that time management only works with action and action and motivation are highly dependent on proper energy management. If you don't manage your energy, then you'll find that you're coming back from your daily class schedule completely wiped out.

Poor energy management is why you end up crashing in front of the TV or staring at your smartphone or computer for hours, and this is one of the key reasons why we don't live life to the fullest! Unfortunately, this goes on to create a negative cycle that makes you even more tired and less energetic because our bodies adapt and become much less efficient. Energy happens at the cellular level; our cells lose mitochondria and become less adept at converting glucose into usable energy. Most people are unaware of this process. People don't routinely think about energy, they don't recognize the importance of energy management, and they certainly are not in the habit of thinking about energy as a finite quantity.

Let's look at how an example of this plays out every day across our great nation. Somebody somewhere this very moment has bought the latest product on how to lose weight and get into shape. They take a look at their current daily activities, and they realize that they're spending a couple of hours in the evening binge-watching Game of Thrones. So, they figure that adding an hour of exercise most evenings shouldn't be a problem, right? So, they come up with an aggressive training program that they think will get the results quickly. Their plan will often include joining a gym, planning on five hours of running/lifting weights a week and probably a 20 or 30-minute commute to and from the gym for each session. At the same time, they will recognize their eating habits stink, so they will change their diet typically reducing their carbohydrate intake. With their new plan in hand, they will be filled with enthusiasm, excitement, and expectations for a quick transformation that lays just around the corner. The approach might sound admirable on paper, but in reality, it's completely delusional!

If you're currently not getting as much exercise as you think you should be, then it probably means that you're too tired, too low on energy and too stressed from the daily grind of school or work or both. If you weren't, then you would likely already be more active in the evenings. If you're currently struggling to do anything in the evenings, what makes you think that you're suddenly going to be able to add five hours of intensive activity out of the gate? And all while consuming fewer carbs which are what give us energy in the first place? Do you see the problem here?

Time is only useful insofar as you have the energy to make use of it and unfortunately, there's no getting around the fact that you need to rest and recuperate. Your plan may be to spend less time chilling in the evening, but unfortunately, the reality is that most of us can't touch that time. Recharging when you're out of energy is sadly not negotiable!

Low energy levels leave you with two real options:

Find ways to increase your energy levels so that you can get more useful hours in the day.

Prioritize by taking other things out of your routine to free up both time and energy for exercise or whatever else it is you want to spend your time on.

Sleeping Habits and Your Energy

Sleep Is Critical

What do you want to do when you feel really tired, and you have no energy left to do anything? You go to sleep.

Your body will tell you quite plainly how important sleep is for energy. In fact, sleep is something of a miracle cure for all kinds of ailments – it improves your memory, your focus, your attention, your mood and your future sleep immensely. Sleeping is far more effective than any beauty treatment, any smart drug, and any supplement. Get the right sleep, and you will be well positioned to perform on the top of your game the next day – it's that simple.

Most of us don't get the quality or the quantity of sleep that we need though, and as such we find ourselves walking around like zombies. We get cranky, we get easily distracted, we get confused, and generally, we operate like shadows of our true selves. So how do you go about upgrading your sleep and recovering from your low energy levels? Let's take a look at some ways to improve your sleep quality.

Tricks to Improve Your Sleep Quality

Take a quick cursory look online, and you'll find that there are thousands of different tips and "hacks" that can supposedly give us better sleep. Everyone it seems has some tip that can lead to amazing sleep, and indeed there are a lot of good ones out there.

But again, some of them involve a lot of work and very little payoff. So instead, let's focus on the tips that will make a noticeable difference and that are relatively easy to implement.

The good news is that if you're following the tips in this book so far, you should already find yourself sleeping much better. That's because you'll have more energy from more efficient mitochondria – and studies show that this is crucial for sleep. It's again something of a vicious cycle: low energy leads to poor sleep, and poor sleep leads to lower energy!

Likewise, if you're eating healthier, you'll be getting the vitamin D, the zinc and magnesium and all kinds of other important nutrients to help your body recover through the night. Finally, if you're reducing your stress, you'll find that this massively has an impact on your ability to sleep as you'll be able to switch off from the stresses of the day much more easily.

Let's look at some specific actions you can easily take to improve your sleep.

How to Calm Your Mind

But what if you're someone who can't sleep? What if your mind is constantly active and you lie in bed with it racing, unable to switch off?

An active mind is a problem a lot of students face, and it can severely rob them of their energy levels the next day. You see, when you lie in bed and try to sleep, you might find that it makes you stressed. The fear of not getting to sleep, or the frustration and the expectation, are so great that they cause you to lie awake worrying. Most of us have had that terrible feeling that occurs when you look at the clock and realize you have to be up in just a few hours and you have not gotten a wink of sleep. An active mind isn't exactly how you sink off to sleep!

To get around this problem then, we're going to take a page out of the CBT book (cognitive behavioral therapy). The idea is to change the way you approach and think about sleep. Specifically, you're going to stop pressuring yourself to sleep and to instead just allow yourself to relax. Consider sleep to be a bonus.

Tell yourself that it's fine to relax in bed and to enjoy being comfy – because it is. That's good for you too. You can't force yourself to sleep, so don't try. Just lie there and enjoy not having to do anything, enjoy not having to be anywhere and enjoy the feeling of closing your eyes and listening to your breathing.

What you'll find, quite ironically, is that as soon as you start taking this approach, you drift right off!

Should You Power Nap?

Even with the best planning and intentions in the world, there will still be times when you don't have the very best sleep and when all your sleeping strategies fail you. In those scenarios, what do you do? Well, one good strategy is to try again later.

You definitely can catch up on some shuteye by power napping and many studies have shown that this can boost productivity, mood and more.

So how do you nap correctly? The secret is to time it correctly and specifically to aim for a minimum of twenty minutes with ninety minutes being ideal, not more and not less. These time bands are important because of the way our body cycles through different stages of sleep (the body loves rhythms!). In 90 minutes, you will go through one complete sleep cycle and will go from the lightest stage of sleep to SWS (slow wave sleep) to REM (rapid eye movements). You'll wake up just as you start to come around. Alternatively, you can sleep for twenty minutes and wake up before you go into the deeper stages of sleep allowing you to avoid sleep inertia. If given a choice, ninety minutes is a more effective solution in boosting our performance.

How the power nap works: Your sleep cycle consists of five stages that recur throughout a typical night of sleep, and a power nap leverages the benefits of the first two cycles. During the first sleep stage, you are sinking into sleep as electrical brain activity, eye and jaw-muscle movement and respiration slow. The second stage is light but restful sleep in which the body gets ready — lowering temperature, relaxing muscles further — for the entry into the deep and dreamless "slow-wave sleep," or SWS, that occurs in stages three and four. Stage five is REM when dreaming becomes intense.

The five sleep stages repeat their cycle every ninety to one hundred and twenty minutes. Stage one can last up to ten minutes, stage two up to the twentieth minute. In addition to improving your alertness and stamina, in stage two, we experience specific electrical signals in the nervous system that solidify the connection between neurons involved in muscle memory making the twenty-minute nap indispensable to the hard-working student looking to recover from a few days of lost sleep.

Take a Hot Bath or Shower Before Bed

A shower is one of the most powerful ways to help yourself sleep more deeply. Taking a hot shower just before you go to sleep will not only relax your muscles, it will also trigger your body to produce growth hormone and melatonin, essentially getting you nice and drowsy.

Have Half an Hour to Rest Before Bed

If there's one life hack that absolutely everyone should subscribe to these days, it's this one. No matter what else is going on in your life: take half an hour before bed to read a book and to relax. Keep your phone off and have just a dim lamp on for reading. Don't watch TV, check social media, or have any deep conversations with your roommate, treat this time as "wind down" time.

This process will allow your mind to start to wind down and allow you to release the stresses of the day and begin to feel more relaxed as a result. Also, the lack of screen time means that your brain will be able to begin producing more melatonin. When you look at a computer or TV screen, your brain interprets the wavelength of the light as being like sunlight. As a result, your brain acts as though it should be daytime, and it floods your body with cortisol, preventing you from sleeping. And this is why it's also so important to make sure there's little light in your room.

The benefits of having half an hour to yourself to unwind go far beyond just better sleep. As a college student, your life is busy, and you never have time to yourself. Often it can feel as though you're are reaching your limits. Start taking time off to decompress, and college and life will seem a lot easier to manage.

Get Into a Routine

Something important to understand about the human body is that it works to rhythms. Your body likes routine because this allows it to learn natural rhythms – highs and lows that will stay consistent ensuring you start winding down biologically at the right moment.

Routines can make a big difference in your ability to doze off, and it will also allow you to control the amount of sleep you're getting more closely. As you likely know, eight hours is a good ball-park figure to aim for if you can. Very few people can function properly on less than six hours sleep a night.

Perfect Your Environment

These are the "easy tips" that pretty much everyone already knows about sleeping – but they're important, and so they're still very much worth going over. Your environment is another key to optimal sleep.

- Since most dorms can be quite loud, use a sleep machine or fan to create white noise and block out as much noise as possible.

- Get your dorm room or apartment as pitch black as possible.

- Keep your room as clean as possible.

- Invest in a mattress topper to make your bed comfortable.

Obviously, it's also very important to wear comfortable sleepwear, to invest in a comfortable bed if you are off campus (one of the best purchases you will ever make) and to keep your room the right temperature. The ideal temperature is for your room to be cool, which is how we are evolutionarily designed to sleep.

In the previous section, we looked at how to get off to sleep and how to ensure we sleep well. That's one part of the story but what comes next is waking up the next day. How do you ensure you can spring out of bed and get lots done?

Your Morning Schedule and Your Energy

How to Wake Up Full of Energy

Now that you know how to get to sleep, the next question is how can you wake up energized. Waking up is the key piece of the puzzle that most people overlook when it comes to sleeping well – but having a good night's sleep does not necessarily mean you'll be able to wake up easily too!

Too many of us wake up feeling groggy, lethargic and tired and as a result, we waste the first half of the day. Some of us will even feel sick in the morning or have bad headaches.

If you fall into this latter category, then, of course, this is not normal, should not be considered "okay" and is something you should discuss with your doctor. A few common culprits for feeling sick, having headaches or feeling "drained" in the morning include:

Dehydration – Try drinking a large glass of water before bed and you won't wake up with a dry throat or a headache.

Low blood sugar – When you go to sleep, you are essentially fasting for 8 hours straight without food. As a result, you can feel sick when you wake up. Some theorists even believe that this is why we have grown to eat dessert as the last meal of the day! Some people recommend having a teaspoon of honey before bed to provide a steady flow of sugar (sucrose and fructose) throughout the night.

Mold – If you have mold in your room this can leave you feeling ill owing to the mycotoxins that it releases. Some signs of mold include a musky smell and damp air. If you notice these things, it can be worth having campus maintenance or a remediation company check things out – even if you can't see mold it can sometimes be building up underneath the floorboards or behind the paint in your rooms!

Allergies – If you're waking up hoarse with a headache, then allergies are a common cause. Even if you don't think you have any allergies, remember that they can come on at any point during your lifetime and as such, you may have developed hay fever or similar allergen. Allergies are especially common if you are going to school out of state as you experience a completely new set of allergens.

Sleep Apnea – Sleep apnea is a condition that causes you to wake up for brief spells during the night because you've stopped breathing. In some cases, this is due to a blocked passage (obstructive apnea), but in others, it may have no cause (primary apnea). The best way to diagnose this is to see a doctor. Bring a video of yourself sleeping, ask a friend to watch you, your doctor will potentially have you visit a sleep clinic. Either way, you might be prescribed a CPAP (continuous positive airway pressure) device which can prevent the problem. If you are snoring, this may be a sign of sleep apnea, be sure to discuss this situation with your doctor.

If you address all these factors, then you should find you start feeling much fresher and more energetic in the morning.

Something else that can help is to look into getting a "daylight lamp." These are lamps that emit a light wave very similar to the sun and which will gradually get brighter in the morning. Daylight lamps can help to gradually nudge you out of a deep sleep rather than waking you in the deepest stages of sleep. At the same time, these lamps can help to combat mild cases of "SAD" (seasonal affective disorder) which is a condition that leaves people feeling tired, lethargic and even potentially depressed during the darker winter months. It can also help to put your biological clock more in-sync with your routine, and in general, it's a very useful tool for waking up more gradually and naturally – it's certainly much better than being startled out of your sleep by a blaring alarm clock.

And another trick you can use that's slightly controversial for waking up in the morning is to use your phone. A lot of people will tell you not to use your phone in the morning to get up, but if you're someone who struggles to wake in the morning, it can be useful. The idea here is to set yourself up to receive something you're looking forward to in the morning – subscribe to some good YouTube channels for instance or join a Facebook community on a subject you're interested. Interesting content will serve as a motivation to get up first thing in the morning to grab your phone. If you can motivate yourself to do just that little bit and to start reading, you'll find that you gradually come around.

There's an App for that – You might also consider using an app that offers sleep tracking. A great example of this would be Sleep Cycle and Pillow. These apps have a great feature which will wake you up out of a light sleep by watching your movement during the night. You set the alarm – say for 7 am – and it waits for a moment near then when you're in light sleep rather than deep sleep. It might go off at 6.30 am for instance, or 6.45 am but never after 7 am. What this means is you're now waking up out of light sleep instead of a heavy sleep which helps to prevent "sleep inertia." In theory, you should be much more awake.

Sleep trackers – can be great for improving energy in other ways too. Some have a constant heart rate monitor which allows you to measure your heart rate throughout the night. Sleep trackers will give you a much more accurate measure of your sleep as well as your calories burned and that in turn will allow you to run experiments to see which sleeping strategies are the most effective for helping you get proper rest.

What to do First?

So, now you're out of bed, what do you do first? A healthy breakfast is a great start to your day and a coffee if you're so inclined (though in the long term, caffeine does more harm than good to energy levels).

Using the tips above you should be feeling fairly awake, but even with the best routines in the world, you'll still potentially feel a little groggy in the morning sometimes and need a bit of help waking up.

One thing that can help you to wake up then is to take a cold shower. A cold shower will not only shock you into wakefulness; it will trigger the release of norepinephrine and dopamine thus making you more alert and even speed up your metabolism to burn more fat. As a way to wake up, this beats a cup of coffee any day!

Next, you'll probably have to head off to class. If you are off campus in a big city, then your commute is one of the very worst things for many when it comes to stress and energy. Not only is it stressful sitting in traffic or on a busy train but it's also a waste of energy. What's more, if you walk on busy streets in the morning, your body will view this as the equivalent of being repeatedly surprised by hundreds of people. Did you know that "things moving toward us" is a universal fear that we all share? Fear and stress can drastically raise your heart rate and make you feel rather exhausted when you get into the classroom.

What's the solution? Live on or very close to campus. Of course, you should look for a less stressful commute if possible but at the very least keep your commute time in mind when thinking about your energy and stress levels and be mindful to stay calm and relaxed.

If you are not running off to class, when starting your day, remember that you're not performing at your absolute optimum when you first get up. A good type of work, to begin with, is something that you can do relatively mindlessly.

When we feel low on energy, exercise can often feel like the last thing we want to do. However, exercising is one of the most powerful ways to boost energy levels in both the very short term and the much longer term.

Exercise and Your Energy

Let's take a look at how exercise improves your energy.

Short Term

In the short term, exercise can give you a great energy boost which is why it's a good way to start your day. One reason that exercising is so good for you in the short term is that it encourages healthy circulation. Exercise gets your heart beating which sends more blood to your muscles and your brain. That means more oxygen and more nutrients which is essentially like getting an injection of rocket fuel!

Exercise also stimulates the release of lots of very positive hormones and neurotransmitters. If you've heard of the "runners-high," then you should know that jogging can stimulate the release of endorphins and serotonin. The result is that you feel very positive, very happy and of course very high in energy.

As a bonus, exercise is also one of the most potent ways to boost the restorative nature of your sleep (we saved this one!). When you work out during the day, you will burn more energy which will mean you will be more likely to doze off at night, especially if you got lots of fresh air by working out outside.

Long Term

But the long-term benefits of exercise are much more profound. For starters, exercise will help you to burn calories and lose weight. Proper weight management means you'll be carrying less weight around with you and will feel lighter, nimbler and far more energetic as a result.

On top of this, exercise will also help to improve your fitness. Improved fitness levels result in a stronger heart and a better VO2 max. VO2 refers to your body's ability to bring in oxygen and to utilize it for energy in a short space of time. A high VO2 max means that you can run long distances without panting or feeling out of breath. Exercise also just so happens to be the perfect antidote to all that sitting in class.

And if you can run a long distance without feeling out of breath then imagine how much easier that walk to class or that hike up to the grocery store will be!

Exercise also builds muscle and believe it or not, that too can help you to feel more energetic. The main reason for this is that it makes various activities less strenuous and tiring – if you've built strong muscles then you'll find lifting things much easier, walking much easier and pretty much everything else much easier too!

112

Better yet, exercise can also boost your mitochondrial count. Your mitochondria are the energy centers of your cells that help you to utilize ATP and to power yourself through your day.

Exercise increases the quantity and efficiency of mitochondria and especially when you use HIIT. HIIT stands for "High-Intensity Interval Training" and is a type of exercise that involves brief bursts of exertion lasting a couple of minutes, followed by longer bursts of active recovery.

So, while some exercise programs might have you running on a treadmill for ten minutes at fifty percent of your maximum capacity, a HIIT workout would involve sprinting on a treadmill for thirty seconds to two minutes, then power walking for three or four minutes, and then sprinting for another thirty seconds two minutes for usually six to eight cycles. This type of exercise has been shown to be more efficient in a shorter time span and is generally a great way to give yourself a boost mentally and physically.

How to Train

Using HIIT is a very good idea if you want to get the most energy benefit in the shortest amount of time. You should also combine this with some weight lifting to get the benefit of more physical strength (and, weightlifting is very good for weight loss and improving your metabolism). I recommend three days of HITT with two days of weight training. You Might schedule HIIT on Monday, Wednesday, and Friday, with weight training on Tuesday, Thursdays. Some students prefer three days of weights, and two days of HIIT, both schedules are effective.

What's also important, is to avoid overdoing your training. Overdoing it is the big mistake that a lot of people make when taking on any new workout routine and it can end up being almost as bad as not exercising at all.

If you lift weights until you are sore for instance, then bear in mind that this now means you're going to be sore for the rest of that day and probably for the next two days. What's the point of being at your physical best if you hurt every time you move? Likewise, if you run too far and too fast, you'll end up feeling too weak and low on energy for the following days and nights. Continue this over-exertion too long, and it can eventually lead to "overtraining" which leaves you feeling tired, listless and upset.

Something to pay attention to here is your heart rate variance. Heart rate variance shows you how well recovered you are after an interval and workout. Make sure you train to the point where it's still fun, to push yourself but not too hard and to listen to what your body is telling you.

Remember - It is important that you visit a doctor before starting any diet or exercising training program.

Your Diet and Your Energy

Diet is one of the biggest contributing factors to low energy, – both for the population in general and for college students specifically.

In the caveman days, we would have eaten a diet that provided us with tons of energy, and that fueled us to chase down prey and to perform at our optimum generally. It is not a coincidence that the food available to us provided us with so much energy and our bodies evolved as they did because of the food that was available. In other words, through thousands of years of evolution, we adapted to thrive on what was available to us.

And now, many of us are surviving on a diet that contains none of that goodness (or at least barely any). Before embarking on any diet, supplement, or exercise plan, visit your doctor to make sure you do so safely.

Our Low Density, Simple Carb Diets

If you're like a lot of people, then you will come home from class after a long, tiring day and you will throw a pizza in the microwave, maybe down something from the university vending machines, or perhaps you'll grab a latte and scone.

Let's take a look at what you get from that. Well, on an energy front you do get a lot of calories. In fact, a standard shop-bought scone will normally land you about 600Kcal. Then you have those chips from the vending machine, they will add in another 200Kcal, your drink, your dessert, still more calories.

By the end, you've no doubt eaten over 1,000 calories, which happens to be half of most people's daily allowance. A poor diet is what's making us fat and carrying all that extra bodyweight around with you is unsurprisingly a surefire way to make yourself tired.

Dumping that much food into your body at once is also not a great move. Now you have a ton of food to process, including low-quality protein, which will slowly move through your digestive system robbing your other functions of energy.

What's more though, the calories you just took in were "simple carbs." The scone, the chips, the desert, the drink, these are simple sugars that spike the bloodstream immediately. And that's before you even count all the added sugar. Suddenly hitting your body with that much raw energy might sound like a good thing for your energy but in fact, you couldn't be further from the truth. Instead, you're spiking your blood sugar, leading to a sudden surge of insulin creating a high. That insulin uses up the sugar and removes it from your blood, but because you're not using it that quickly, it simply gets stored as fat (a process called lipogenesis). And guess how you feel once that process has ended? Exhausted! And you get a sudden energy slump (which by the way, is when most of us snack on more sugar).

Worse yet, all those calories and simple carbs have done you approximately zero good. Why? All the scone consists of is flour and sugar, the chips offer no nutritious value. So, all you're doing every day is dumping your body full of low-quality food to process and in vast quantities. Is it no wonder why you are tired?

Supplements That Provide Energy

Now, I could tell you to cut it out. To stop eating that garbage and to start eating healthily again. But it wouldn't do any good.

How can I be sure of that? Because you already knew that your diet probably wasn't all that healthy. You already know that home-cooked fresh ingredients are much better.

The problem? You don't have the time, energy or perhaps even money to change the way you eat. Notice that energy is a problem here: something of a vicious circle, isn't it?

So, to jumpstart your self-improvement and your drive towards more energy, why don't we start with a supplement stack? The following ingredients are things you can take with your meals which will greatly enhance your energy levels:

Vitamin D is excellent for two things: improving your sleep and helping you to produce more testosterone. The vast majority of us are deficient, so take this in the morning, and you'll start feeling a lot better.

Iron and Vitamin B12 are required to give us our healthy red blood cells. In case you forgot, red blood cells are the oxygen-carrying portion of our blood which our body uses to burn fat and fuel all kinds of processes in our body.

Omega 3 Fatty Acid is an essential fatty acid that the body uses to create cell walls. Increasing your cell membrane permeability is very important. Why? Because it helps the cells to communicate with one another and it allows neurotransmitters to pass more easily between brain cells.

Creatine is a supplement used by athletes. Its job is to take the broken-down form of ATP (adenosine triphosphate) and recombine it for extra use in the body. What does this mean? Well, ATP is the main energy currency of all life. It comes from glucose and releases energy when the bonds connecting three molecules break apart. This results in ADP (adenosine diphosphate) and AMP (adenosine monophosphate) – a two for one. Normally that's all the use you can get out of it, but with creatine, you can reuse the energy by re-bonding the ADP and AMP back together.

The body produces creatine naturally, but if you take it in supplement form, you can get a little more. In real terms, this means a few extra seconds of exertion when lifting weights or running a marathon – and it means better mental energy for performing your school work and fighting the daily stresses of college life.

Lutein is generally thought of as a supplement for the eyes to help prevent macular degeneration. Recent studies suggest it could also enhance the performance of the mitochondria – the energy factories that live inside each of our cells. When given to mice, they would voluntarily run miles further each week on their treadmills – pointing to increased energy and performance.

Garlic Extract is a vasodilator. Vasodilator means that it can widen the blood vessels to allow more blood and oxygen to get around – to the brain and muscles for instance - thus fueling you with more energy.

Vitamin B6 is used to help us extract energy from carbohydrates. At the same time, B6 helps with the creations of neurotransmitters which helps it to boost cognitive performance. Low levels of B6 have been shown to result in lack of energy and focus and even shrinking brain tissue and Alzheimer's.

Coenzyme Q10 is another substance that athletes are very interested in at the moment and which can considerably increase the efficiency of the mitochondria for enhanced fat burning and energy production.

The Perfect Diet

Now that's a lot of different supplements to be taking. It's quite a long shopping list, and it would get pretty expensive. Here's the thing though: you needn't be taking any of these supplements. Not if your diet is correct.

All of these things can be found in your diet if you know where to look. CoQ10 and creatine are in red meats, vitamins and minerals are in all our fruits and vegetables, omega three fatty acids is in fish, lutein is in eggs.

If you make sure that everything you're eating is fresh and nutritious, then you'll be providing your body with all the energy it needs. You'll be able to absorb it better, and you'll be getting it in the right ratios and quantities. Meanwhile, other substances found in your diet can help to boost your energy levels as well: zinc, magnesium, vitamin C, PQQ, l-carnitine, l-theanine, and resveratrol are just a few. Eating a healthy diet is like having an incredibly expensive athlete's supplement stack! Only better.

Meanwhile, you should try to avoid the "simple" carbs. That's anything that tastes sweet (like cake) and anything white (like pasta or rice). Instead, start eating brown rice, and pasta, vegetables, spinach and have that in the place of your chips (as a rule, try to avoid processed, human-made carbs). Proper nutrition will allow the body to release energy much more slowly and provide you with a steady supply throughout the day. Don't be afraid of fat either – it contains more calories (9 per gram versus 4), but it's slow release too. Try to eat smaller portions, more often and don't over-stuff yourself.

How do you go about cooking these nutritious, fresh meals when you lack time and energy? A good plan is to prepare your meals at the start of the week. Cook up a few pots of food you can dip into throughout the week and keep what you don't eat in the freezer or plastic containers. If you purchased your universities meal plan, you generally could save time by cutting out the shopping and preparation time. Most universities now provide healthy and well-balanced meal options, if you have the willpower to skip the dessert bar! A few students report they hate cooking because their roommates expect them to prepare food for them as well. If you live on campus in a dorm, a meal plan is likely your best choice. Most universities meal plans include dollars to eat at your on-campus Chick-Fil-A, Starbucks, Panera, or national food chain of choice.

On Going Too Far

We eat too many processed carbs. And if we ate less of those carbs, we'd feel much better. At the same time though, we still need carbs. They're still an important food group in our diet, and if we get the right kind in the right quantities, they boost testosterone production and aid with our general levels of energy and well-being. Restrict carbs too much, and you'll feel tired. The occasional bit of brown pasta with your bolognese won't kill you. In fact, many old-school bodybuilders eat nothing but rice and steamed chicken when training for competition.

Likewise, while natural, unprocessed foods are healthier than cake, pie, and chips, you don't need to eat only the things you would find in caveman days. A lot of serious Paleo dieters will tell you not to eat bread, wheat or cheese. And they will never break their diet to have a bowl of pasta.

But here's the thing: most of the top performing athletes in the world have performed just fine on bread. Some of the smartest thinkers in the world drank lots of tea and ate lots of chocolate.

Point being? You can perform just fine eating a relatively "normal" diet. And, our lifestyle places different demands on our body these days anyway; it's only natural our diet should adjust. In other words, don't waste your energy thinking you can only eat specific foods. Start with your current diet but make it a little healthier by cutting back on the simple carbs and by injecting more nutrients. As you feel the results, you will find your body will crave the junk less, and before you know it, your diet will be quite healthy. There is some emerging research that indicates gluten-free diets may have a significant impact on the long-term positive brain function. As diet science constantly evolves, it makes sense to approach your nutrition and diet with a grain of salt, and practice moderation in your approaches. Pay attention to how your body responds to your diet and adjust accordingly. Make sure to get an annual physical that includes blood work as it is essential to consult your physician before making changes to your diet, taking supplements, or starting an exercise program.

Habits and Lifestyle Impact Your Energy

Once you've upgraded your diet, you'll find that you immediately start feeling more energetic. Diet is a critical part of the battle. But really to improve your energy, you need to look at the bigger picture.

No part of our health exists in a vacuum, and even the best diet in the world can't stand up to the wrong lifestyle or the wrong routine.

In fact, you're probably doing a bunch of things right now that are completely ruining your energy levels. If you can find these energy black holes, then you'll be able to save yourself large packets of energy to use in other, more constructive ways throughout the day.

Alcohol and Your Energy

Here comes the bad news alcohol is very bad for your energy levels. As in, it's down-right awful.

In the short term, alcohol is terrible for your energy and can leave you completely exhausted. Alcohol is a depressant, which means that it works to inhibit the firing of neurons in your brain, slowing down your thinking and making you sleepy. Alcohol, like a sleeping pill or anxiolytic, works the opposite of a stimulant. And because it causes whole areas of the brain to stop working, it can rob you of your higher order brain function too.

If you are planning on being productive – think twice about picking up that beer or glass of wine. Drinking alcohol also has longer-term effects on your energy levels and general health. Of course, alcohol also contributes to weight gain at seven calories per gram. It can cause headaches the next day, and it significantly impairs the quality of your sleep. Try wearing a heart rate monitor when you drink alcohol, and you'll see it sends it sky-high, which isn't exactly conducive to a restful night! Although alcohol is a depressant, it amps up the body as it tries to purge what is essentially a toxin from your system.

If you're going to drink alcohol, try to have your last glass a few hours before bed. And try eating a banana and honey sandwich as a hangover cure. It can work wonders as the banana and honey will line the stomach, replenish your energy stores, fix your electrolytes and break down acetaldehyde – a toxic substance that is responsible for a lot of the negative effects associated with a hangover.

Water

So, if you shouldn't be drinking alcohol, what you should be drinking is water.

Water is crucial to your energy levels as it's what the body uses for pretty much every crucial function. You've probably read stats telling you that your body is seventy percent water or there about and it's true – you are mostly water.

Too bad then that the majority of the US population are chronically dehydrated! Dehydration leads to headaches, cramps, dry throats and of course – tiredness.

How much water should you be drinking? A good guide is to try and consume at least seven to ten glasses a day. Try this, and you should find that you start feeling energized. And remember, dehydration kills your cognitive function by up to 30%.

Sitting Too Much

As a student, the simple fact of the matter is that you probably sit far too much. You are sitting in class, sitting in the library, sitting in your dorm, etc.

Sitting is bad for us for all kinds of reasons. The main one though is that it's terrible for our hearts – the longer you spend sitting during the day, the more health issues you are likely to develop over the longer-term.

Stress Management

Sitting for long durations is bad, but potentially more destructive is stress, which is something that a great many of us experience on campus and the job. If you are very stressed at school, then you should not underestimate just what a severe impact this can have on your health, your mood, and your energy levels.

The idea of stress is to increase our awareness, our physical strength and our ability to think quickly. Thus, when we are stressed, our bodies respond by releasing dopamine, norepinephrine and other "fight or flight" hormones. The chemical releases in your body increase your heart rate; directs more blood flow to the muscles and the brain, and it heightens our awareness. At the same time, we might start trembling, our immune systems and digestive systems become suppressed, and we'll feel anxious and jittery.

All these effects are designed to help us in a fight or flight situation. In other words, they are meant to come on fast and be over quickly. If we saw a predator or prey, if we fought with someone, or if we saw a fire – then this would be exactly how the fight or flight system would work and, it would probably help us to stay alive.

Today though, stress is not acute – it is chronic. Our modern sources of stress include things like exams, projects, papers, angry bosses, poor finances, strained relationships, and looming deadlines; all these are things that have no finite end, or no imminent end at least. In other words, our body is constantly in this state of arousal, and as such, our immune system is constantly suppressed leaving us susceptible to illness. Likewise, so too is our digestion, robbing us of the nutrients we should be getting from our food.

And eventually, the brain will run low on those fight or flight hormones. At this point, your sympathetic nervous system burns out, and you reach a point known as adrenal fatigue. It's then that you will find yourself robbed of the neurotransmitters that normally help you to get up in the morning and to focus on the task at hand. And without these neurotransmitters, you will feel demotivated, low on energy and listless – low levels of neurotransmitters lead to depression.

So, if you're getting to that point where you have no energy in the morning and where it's all just starting to feel a little bit too hard to carry on – you're probably experiencing adrenal fatigue as a result of stress.

If you are in that situation, then it's highly advisable that you change some aspect of your lifestyle or your routine. While it might not be easy to change your major or transfer schools, to take time out of a relationship, or to speak to a counselor – it's crucial that you take positive actions. Ultimately, your health and your quality of life are what you should be putting first - above all else.

Using all the advice we've covered so far in this book, you should now be reaching the point where you are well prepared to manage your time, schedule, and energy. Even with this knowledge though, it's important to realize that you still aren't completely in charge of everything and you're still in some ways restricted by higher forces.

Specifically, your energy will rise and fall with your body's natural rhythms. Your energy levels ebb and flow like waves, and at some points, you are going to be high in energy, and at other points, you are going to be low in energy. Energy levels are set partly by your internal body clock (internal pacemaker) and partly by external cues (external zeitgebers) such as social cues, eating habits and light.

In the morning when you wake up, your body is flooded with cortisol and this helps you to start shifting into first gear. Your energy then remains fairly steady until lunch, when you replenish your glucose stores and then again at 4 pm at which point you will reach a low point in your natural energy cycle. 4 pm is when many of us start feeling sleepy and wanting to curl up on the couch. We also feel tired after eating food while we're digesting, so if you eat a meal at 3.30pm, you may as well write 4 pm off completely.

Your energy will improve after 4 pm but will slowly tail off until bedtime. There will be another slump, peak, and slump following dinner.

Structuring Your Day for Optimum Productivity

Simply knowing that these ebbs and flows exist and knowing when you're going to be performing your best can help a great deal with your ability to stay productive and to get the most out of yourself.

Another tip is to avoid having big plans after dinner. If you have anything productive to do, then do it before you eat. The minute you eat dinner and sit on the couch, your energy will be in decline, and your ability to be productive will decline significantly.

Ebbs and flows apply on a larger scale as well. Specifically, you will find that you also have months where energy is high and months where you struggle. This ebb and flow can impact your exercise – you can have months of being highly disciplined and training well, and then have months of low energy or a felling you have plateaued. Don't punish yourself when this happens, go with your body's natural inclination and try to plan tasks for the points in time when you are most likely to be able to focus on and complete them.

Individual Differences and How to Control Your Cycles

We've looked at the times you're most likely to be productive or sleepy during the day, and for most people, this will ring true. However, keep in mind that everyone is different. Some people are night owls and are more productive later at night, while other people are early birds and will tend to get their best work done first thing in the morning when the rest of us are still groggy and experiencing sleep inertia. Pay attention to your energy levels throughout the day and learn your cycles and work to optimize your schedule within those natural rhythms continually.

At the same time, remember that you can control your rhythms to help your energy cycles sync up with what you're doing at any given time. The daylight lamp we mentioned earlier is one, and another is to time when you eat carefully. Not only can changing your eating schedule help you move that after-dinner slump but it also actually affects your body clock. Eat dinner later, and you'll find it a little easier to sleep later. Daytime naps can also help with this.

Throughout this book, we've covered a lot of different points, and right now your mind might be swimming with ideas for how to get more energy and how to change your routine for the better.

To help you cement all these ideas then, let's quickly recap on some of the tools and strategies you can now be using to get more energy:

Start eating more healthily

- Avoid processed foods
- Avoid simple carbohydrates
- Eat nutrient dense foods
- Eat smaller meals, more regularly
- Eat complex carbs that release energy more slowly
- Don't get too carried away with fad diets
- Prepare meals in advance
- Supplement if necessary

Exercise more

- Use HIIT training to increase mitochondria
- Don't overtrain

Manage your sleep

- Have half an hour to relax in the evenings
- Take a hot shower before bed

Wake up slowly

- Use a sleep tracker
- Tempt yourself out of bed with something interesting
- Take a cold shower!

Plan your day to coincide with your natural energy highs and lows

- Do productive things first
- Time meals to adjust your body clock

Learn what works for you!

All of this might sound like quite a lot and especially if you're feeling low on energy. If you're exhausted right now, then can you be bothered to take up a new exercise program? Can you find the energy to bike to class? How will you ever find the time to change your whole routine? Find time to cook these fresh, healthy meals?

All these strategies might sound like a lot, and it might sound daunting, but that's why it can pay to keep in mind the Japanese principle of Kaizen. Kaizen means making small, incremental changes that all add up to something big and profound. It is like the Magic Penny doubling each day to create millions.

A small step, like swapping your morning donut and coffee for a smoothie, and experiencing how much more energy you get from this small change will build momentumn. It's a very small change but it will make a huge difference, and you will find it very motivating.

If you can't commit to half an hour of winding down in the evening, try making it ten minutes. If you can't commit to twenty minutes of meditation, do five minutes.

And if working out five days a week is too daunting, commit to half an hour twice a week, to begin. You get the idea.

In fact, this strategy of small incremental changes is the exact game plan coach Pat Riley used with the Los Angeles Lakers to win the NBA Championship in the1987-1988 season. During the previous season, the team had self-destructed during the Western Conference Finals, losing to Houston. Coach Riley spent the summer uncovering what went wrong, where they would need to improve their game to win the championship. Coach Riley and his staff identified five areas that each player on the team needed to improve.

During training camp for the next season, coach challenged each player to improve one percent above the career best in each of five areas. One percent doesn't seem like much, but if you take a dozen players on the team and each improves one percent in five areas, the team gains a whopping 60% improvement in overall performance.

Because the players saw one percent as very achievable, they were able to focus their efforts on small, realistic actions to improve. The results were amazing with most players improving double digits, and one player improved an amazing 50 percent. The individual improvements translated to 67 team wins and an NBA Championship.

The following season the team would repeat as champions becoming the first team in nineteen years to win back-to-back titles.

Small, focused changes can go a long way on your road to success. And whether your goal is to win an NBA Championship, land that perfect job, or launch your own business, ultimately applying small changes and watching them compound over time will lead to massive success. **And it all starts with just one small change!**

Managing Work and Fun

"Never get so busy making a living that you forget to make a life." — Dolly Parton

Working While in College

For many college students, having to hold down a part-time or even full-time job is one of the difficult realities of the modern education system. Every student's financial situation is different and very few students have parents with an endless supply of cash. Many students need to work to get by, and still, others choose to earn their own money to reduce their need for financial aid or scholarships. So how do you balance your job with everything else?

Communicating your daily class schedule is at the top of the list. Be sure your boss knows your class schedule and have a heart-to-heart with him or her about your time needs. Many workplaces are sympathetic to the plight of the working college student. Communication is essential to having a successful co-existence with your job and your schooling.

Many family-owned businesses tend to be much more understanding of the college student and are willing to work with employees who are full-time students.

Consider finding work on campus. Check the bulletin boards, websites, career office, etc., for jobs that will fit into your schedule or find the human resources department and inquire about available positions. Many colleges offer work in your field of study, which could prove to be invaluable. Working on campus eliminates travel time to an outside job and minimizes the stress of trying to coordinate classes with your job.

Don't try to take on too many hours in any given semester. Studies show that students who work more than 15 hours at a part-time job while carrying a full load of classes experience more stress and have a larger chance of dropping out of school due to that stress. While it's important to have the income to offset expenses, it's also important to concentrate on your studies.

Take advantage of downtime. When you have a break, review your notecards. During your lunch or dinner break, read a chapter while eating a sandwich. Talk to your employer about studying during lulls while on the clock. If you work at, say, a retail store, see if your boss would be willing to allow you to study in between customers. When you take advantage of the time available your success at balancing work and studies will increase greatly.

Working while in college offers the student more than just the chance to make money. Campus jobs allow students to work with faculty and administrators who can often serve as mentors. And students can often find jobs that relate to their academic work (lab work, research, etc.). Just as importantly, campus jobs often provide students with the opportunity to examine various career options. At the very least, potential employers appreciate the fact that students worked while they were in college.

Don't be afraid to let your professors know that you have a job. Most teachers have learned to turn a deaf ear to students with poor excuses for not doing their assignments on time, but that doesn't mean they aren't willing to make exceptions when they know the need is there.

Although working while in college is important, it's not for everyone. Working, like the rest of one's college experiences, must be kept in perspective. Working should be a complement rather than a hindrance to the student's academic activities. Try it -- if it doesn't work or if academic problems occur, talk with your academic dean. Immediately!

If working gets to be too much, consider other routes for earning cash, or modify your budget. You should NEVER let work hold you back from achieving your dream of a college education. There are many resources available. Take advantage of them! Use them! Go to the financial aid office and discuss your situation with a counselor there. You might be surprised by the options available.

Consider some of these other tips:

- Get a work-study job if you are eligible. The Federal Work-Study Program offers jobs to eligible Federal financial aid recipients. If you receive Federal financial aid, your award letters will identify whether you are eligible for work-study and the number of hours you will be allowed to work.

- If you are eligible, you can then go to your financial aid office and apply for available work-study jobs. These jobs can either be on campus or off campus and are usually at a non-profit organization or public agency. These organizations generally let students work very flexible hours.

- Get a job that includes tips. Jobs with wages plus tips often pay the best. So, if you are looking to earn more money while in college, consider being a waiter, waitress or bartender at a local restaurant. Just keep in mind that these job hours may not be as flexible as a job on campus or a work-study job.

- Advertise your services. If you like to type or edit papers or tutor other students, why not get paid for it? Put up posters around campus that show students what you are offering and how much you charge. Post on university social media accounts, and local online resources.

No matter what route you take to make more money, try to find one that doesn't interfere too much with your schoolwork. If you are having trouble finding the time to go to class or to do your homework, try cutting back on your hours at work.

Another component of reducing stress and maximizing your time is effectively managing your money. Whether it comes from mom and dad or your hard-earned paycheck, money management for college students is essential to learn.

Money Tips

Money certainly makes the world go round, and we all need to be mindful of how much money we have and where all of it is going. Money management is especially necessary for college students. College expenses are ridiculously high with tuition, books, fees, parking, room and board, rent, gas, date money, movie rentals, etc. Effective money management is made easier with these tips.

First, track your spending for two to four weeks to find out where your money is going. Ask yourself if seven or eight trips to Starbucks a week is really necessary? You probably don't realize how much money you spend on little things like snacks and drinks. Often, just by tracking expenses, you'll start to curb your expenses and spend your money more effectively.

The best way to manage your money over the course of a semester is to sit down and map out a budget. List sources of income such as scholarships, loans, money from summer jobs, and cash from your parents. Then list your expenses, such as tuition, books, and groceries. If your income is larger than your spending, you're on the right track!

Going to buy new clothes, going to a concert, or movie... make room for that in your budget. After all, you do need some fun and entertainment in your life. You'll get burned out if you don't have any fun. But be mindful of your entertainment expenses so that they don't get out of hand.

If you spend, spend, spend at the beginning of the semester, you will be broke later in the term. Give yourself a spending limit for each week. Stick to it, and you won't have to eat macaroni-and-cheese every day in December.

Be careful with credit card use. Having a credit card is a good idea in case of emergencies, but having that little piece of plastic can make your spending get way out of control, very, very quick. One quick way to spend beyond your means is to charge it. Use credit cards sparingly. Once you get into the habit of reaching for plastic, it can be hard to stop.

Keep only one credit card. You'll receive countless offers from credit card companies wanting to give you credit at recklessly high-interest rates to celebrate your arrival into the "real world." Find a card with a low-interest rate and use it as little as possible. And don't charge small purchases! You don't want to be paying interest on a cup of coffee!

If you're afraid you'll keep spending as long as there's room on the card, call your credit card company and request your credit limit be lowered. Keep at it. Card companies will try to boost up your credit lines, so you spend more. Just say "no" each time they try.

Be realistic about your spending habits. You can do what you want, but you can't do everything you want. You're going to have to make some choices. Whatever you choose it is going to cost some money. You need to understand you can't have everything and you have to understand there are consequences.

If you bust your budget on something you want to do this week, make up for it next week. If you go out to dinner and a movie one week, spend the money; be satisfied with the decision, and commit to staying home, eating at home, and not making any other purchases the following week.

Plan for big expenses. Whether it's a road trip with friends or a car insurance bill, if you know a big expense is coming, start putting some money aside to pay for it. It's a lot easier to set aside $50 every month than to come up with $600 when the bill is due.

When it comes to dorm or apartment expenses, contact your roommate before the semester starts and divvy up expenses. Decide who will bring a refrigerator and who will bring a microwave, etc. This way you avoid duplicating purchases and excess spending but will allow you to have all the conveniences still to make college life easier.

Most of the big expenses are at the beginning of the school year. Don't forget to check out prices from online bookstores. They may give you a better deal than the campus bookstore. Buy used books whenever possible. Check Amazon, e-bay or half.com with the ISBN of the textbooks you need. You can usually get this number from your college bookstore, and the prices are usually a lot lower than what the bookstore will charge.

Don't forget, too, that when the semester is over if you have a book you don't think you'll use ever again – Thermonuclear Dynamics, The History of the Hobbit, etc. – sell them back to the school or list them online. Selling your books can be a really easy way to make a little cash at the end of the semester.

Get help earlier rather than later. It's very difficult to say, "I'm in trouble and I need $2,000" or "I spent my student loan money on an awesome spring break trip." The longer you put it off, the worse things will get. While your parents might not be thrilled that you've been so careless with your money, I'm willing to bet that they'll probably be ready to help you out – after a lecture and tongue lashing of course!

Remember that money management is really about resource management. Also, know that money usually operates within us on at least two different levels. There is the practical dimension from which we make purchases. There is also the symbolic level. Money can buy us pleasure, friendships, or give us the feeling of power. We need to be careful not to let money substitute for emotional needs we need to address in other ways.

If money is a little tight, there are some easy things you can do every day to save and avoid the money crunch.

- Don't eat fast food every day. Look into the meal plans offered by the school's cafeteria. Buy quick, convenient things to make in your room.

- Use coupons for things you frequently buy; keep them in your car so that they are handy for the store, fast food or restaurants.

- Stream a movie instead of going out to a movie theater.

- Consolidate errands to cut down on extra gasoline expenses. When you do buy gas, do it at a gas station that has competition close by to increase your likelihood of getting the lowest price.

- Stock up at holiday and back-to-school sales for things you know you will need later.

- Consider a new cell phone plan or even switching companies if you can save money by doing so.

- Use a shopping list when at the store; do not deviate from your list whenever possible.

- Keep your eye on the register when checking out at stores, purchases can easily scan incorrectly.

One final note, as crazy as it may seem, because college is a time of money shortages, consider the idea of putting a little money away on a weekly basis. Two dollars a week at the end of the year is still a hundred and four dollars. Then do something extraordinarily nice for yourself or with someone else.

Saving is a part of spending too. See if these brief money-managing tips might not help you achieve your goals and objectives in college. It is often said, "If you manage your time, you manage your life. If you waste your time, you waste your life." With money, perhaps we should be saying, "Manage it, don't let it manage you." Now let's move on to the fun stuff – enjoying yourself, making time for fun, and getting the most out of college life!

Party Responsibly

Parties and socializing are a big part of student life on campus. And contrary to some people thoughts, you should not deny yourself the right to enjoy the non-academic side of the university. However, every semester, some students are placed on probation or kicked out of school due to poor decisions and actions taken while under the influence. You should keep in mind, that partying is only a small part of the college experience. It has its pitfalls, and you need to be careful that you don't overdo it so that it negatively affects your goals and future.

When you have an early class, avoid the bars the night before. You're just setting yourself up for trouble if you don't. Even if you do get up the next morning after a late night out, you won't be able to focus on your classes. The lack of focus will result in missing important information that you will need later on. Also, you won't be performing to your full potential if you're tired or hung over.

Be mindful of the downfalls of excessive alcohol use. I am not saying you have to avoid alcohol completely. If you're of legal age and you want to enjoy a drink or two, by all means, go ahead. But, it's easy for a few drinks to turn into a few more and before you know it, you've developed a problem. Warning signs that alcohol may be a problem include:

- Missing classes or appointments
- Declining grades
- Aggressive behavior while drunk
- Erratic behavior while drinking
- Blacking out or poor recollection of events
- Drinking when under stress

If you think you might have a problem, don't hesitate to seek help. Most college campuses have counselors on staff to help with problems affecting college students. Talk to your family doctor or attend an Alcoholics Anonymous meeting.

Never, ever, drink and drive. Take an Uber, Lyft, or cab, take turns with your friends being designated driver, or walk (but be careful – you CAN get a ticket for public intoxication if you're too smashed!) Safety should be first and foremost in your mind – at all costs! Bad things do happen both on and off campus, always be safe and stay with a group.

There's much more to college life than partying, though. Enjoy the other aspects of the university. Join an organization that seems interesting and where you will find like-minded students. Were you student body president in high school? Look into student council or get involved in campus politics. If you're interested in acting, consider student theater productions, interested in business, technology, marketing, there is a club for that. Most colleges have hundreds of clubs ranging from soccer to science, spend some time on your universities website and check out clubs on display during orientation and other times of the year on campus.

Sororities and fraternities are present on most four-year campuses. These are great places to make new friendships that can last for a lifetime. There's often a "rush" week during which time you can visit the houses and learn more about which groups you might want to join.

Often, there is a voting process during which you will be accepted or rejected. Don't be discouraged if things don't work out on your first try. It is not a personal statement on your worth. Just don't give up. Being part of a fraternity or sorority can be great fun and a huge learning experience.

Don't discount laid-back activities as well. Simply watching a movie or playing video games with your dorm-mates can be great relaxation and just as fun as going to a bar – but without the hangover!

Having fun is a big part of college life. You deserve to enjoy the whole experience, so be sure and make time for yourself and developing friendships and new interests.

So, what if you're a non-traditional student? Think this advice doesn't apply to you? Let's address that in our next section.

Tips for Non-traditional Students

Many older adults are going back to college to complete degrees they started years ago, to fulfill a lifelong ambition, or to train for a new career path. Time management for non-traditional students is especially crucial as the issue of children and family contributes to the already hectic life of a full-time college student. Some non-traditional students also juggle full-time jobs along with their studies. Finding time to study, take care of a home, work an outside job, and have a personal life seems out of reach. However, time management skills make it not only possible but also realistic.

Refer to the section in this book regarding using your planner. With other activities going on in your lives, having a planner and referring to it often is more crucial than ever. You will also want to invest in a dry erase board for your home in a calendar format to keep track of events, appointments, and homework assignments. Calendaring can be especially helpful so that your family always knows where you are. Keep the board in a convenient, well referred to place such as the refrigerator or by the front door.

Use a different color marker for each family member, so you know who is where and when. List your class schedule on the dry erase board and have your family members record their activities along with times to keep track of everyone's schedule. It's a good idea to copy this same schedule down in your planner since your planner should always be with you and you will always know how to schedule your hectic life.

Remember why you are in college in the first place and make this a priority in your life. It's essential that you talk with family and friends to ensure they understand that even though they do matter tremendously to you, your school work is a priority and their support is needed.

Allot a specific time each day for studying. You need a quiet place with minimal distractions. You may want to physically write your study schedule on the dry erase board as well. Let your family know that when you're studying, you must be left alone. Then do nothing else during that time. Shut off the phone, stay put, and concentrate on your studies.

Organization skills are another key component to effective time management. While we do have a whole section in this book on organization, some special attention needs to be taken to address your special circumstances. You need to identify one specific place to keep all your books and reference materials. Keep a separate bag or backpack to hold that day's books and anything you will need for class.

When you study, designate a separate study space where you can be away from your family. The key is to eliminate all distractions and focus on your schoolwork. Make sure you keep a supply of paper and pencils nearby this space as well.

Take advantage of "down" time. You can study on your lunch break at work, while watching your child's soccer game, sitting in the doctor's office, or anywhere you have waiting time. Of course, in your car commuting to class is probably a bad idea!

You might be apprehensive and even nervous about returning to school, but realize that this is a normal reaction. You're returning to a setting you haven't seen in a while, and when you get there, you'll be with much younger people, which can seem overwhelming. Don't feel alone. Look around the campus. I'd bet you're not the only one there.

Chances are, the traditional college student won't care that you're older than they are. Once the class is in full swing and your part of the class environment, you may be surprised when some of those younger students come to you for help and advice.

Take advantage of all the resources your college has to offer such as computer labs, library resources, help centers, and tutors. Don't be afraid to ask for help – especially from your professors. If you do not understand something in the class, arrange a meeting when your professor has office hours. Most instructors are more than willing to help out their students – especially the non-traditional ones!

Almost every college has a program for the non-traditional student that helps with adjusting to college life, honing your study skills, and dealing with the pressures of juggling studies, family, and work. Use these services as they are designed to help YOU!

You Got This!

"If You Can Dream It, You Can Do It." — *Walt Disney*

Whether you're embarking on your college career just out of high school or later in life, time and energy management and all that goes with it is a very important aspect of a successful college experience. If you control your time, you control your stress, and you allow yourself to be positioned to perform to the best of your abilities.

There are so many aspects of a college education that rely on positively managing your time, your money, and your life. While it might seem overwhelming at first, if you tackle one thing at a time, it will be much more manageable and easier to achieve the goals that you set for yourself.

Keep your eye on the "prize." Never forget why you're in college and remember that with the right tools, you can achieve your dreams. Refer to this book often. It is a gathering of personal experience, time-honored tips from the pros, and practical advice that works.

In June 2005, Steve Jobs took the podium at Stanford Stadium to give the commencement speech to Stanford's graduating class. Wearing jeans and sandals under his formal robe, Jobs addressed a crowd of 23,000 with a short speech that drew lessons from his life. About a third of the way into the address, Jobs offered the following advice: "You've got to find what you love...the only way to do great work is to love what you do. If you haven't found it yet, keep looking, and don't settle."

When it comes to your impulses, desires, and goals, you can either control them – and your destiny – or you can let them control you. Anyone – including you – can reach their goals and find success and happiness. Whatever you want out of life – be it fame, fortune, power, or impact, you can achieve it. Whether you want to be a rock star, a successful entrepreneur or have a wonderful, loving family, it is all within your reach. But be careful, what we think we want and what we truly desire are often two very different things. So, you need to figure out what you want and then get ready to go for it.

Setting and achieving goals is one of the most exciting and fulfilling things that you can do in your life. There is very little that compares with the thrill of sitting back one day and realizing that the goals you set your freshman year – the ones that you never thought you would be able to achieve are not only within grasp, but have already happened. You then realize you barely noticed that you reached your goals because you were already planning the next ones.

If you are going to dream – then dream big and then put everything you have into realizing that dream. At first, your goals will seem like a distant star; the stars seem a billion miles away. But if you keep reaching for your goals with everything you have, eventually you will build momentum, and the compound effect will ignite you like a rocket heading to space. From that rocket ship, you will find your goals pluck right out of the night sky. All you have to do is create a sound plan, make an effort, and give yourself enough time to reach your dreams.

I hope that this book will give you the foundation and confidence to chase your dreams. All you need to do is choose a dream. So, stop waiting. College is your moment!

Before you know it, you'll be walking across that stage again and collecting a diploma – only this time, it will say "College Graduate" - You Got This!

Conclusion and Invitation

Learn from the mistakes of others. You can't live
long enough to make them all yourself
— Eleanor Roosevelt

WOW! I'm sure by now you're probably feeling like you have been drinking from a fire hose, and I understand that.

Like me, you were probably shocked to learn that only around half of the students who enroll in college end up graduating with a bachelor's degree and that **30% of college freshman dropout after their first year.**

The system is clearly not working! Being successful at college requires a full range of skills. Some come into play at key moments in the semester, like when you're facing major tests and papers. Other skills will help you rise to the top throughout the semester. Let's face it, on most days you must go to class, do the assigned reading, and study for some weekly quiz. That's why it's important to have all the skills of college down cold.

Time Management is a core skill, but it is not the only skill you need to be successful in college.

If you study, learn, adapt, and grow, you will come out of college with not only a degree but with the skills to launch you at the start of a successful career.

For many college students, this may seem more like a dream than a reality. Sure, they've learned the basics – the first level of studying, managing their time and taking a test that just about everyone learns in high school. Some have even mastered an intermediate level of skills that, with luck, they learned early in their college career. But you want advanced, fully polished, professional-level skills that'll drive you to the top of your class and lead to a great career.

My goal is to help you achieve the success you want, and that is why I founded College Success Academy. My mission is to help millions of high school seniors and underclassmen successfully transition to college and become more self-reliant, fulfilled, and successful.

With that goal in mind, I developed a complete college success system, which allows you to hit campus ready to go just like a seasoned upperclassman. In this program, **you will learn:**

- ✓ How to Demystify the College Experience
- ✓ How You Can Prevent Academic Problems
- ✓ How to Manage Your Grade Point Average
- ✓ Classroom Skills to Boost Your GPA
- ✓ Top Study Skills of the Best Students
- ✓ Test-Taking Skills for Racking Up A's
- ✓ Paper-Writing Skills
- ✓ How to Take Effective Notes
- ✓ Secrets Hidden in Your Professors Syllabus
- ✓ The Secrets Top Students Know

- ✓ Time Management Skills and Strategies
- ✓ Mastering Procrastination
- ✓ Winning Strategies for Interacting with Your Professors
- ✓ Managing Stress
- ✓ Leveraging Technology

…And Much, Much More!

As a reader of this book, I have created a unique opportunity for you to learn how you can create your own unfair advantage in college and achieve the success you deserve. Just visit www.IwantSuccessInCollege.com to learn more.

Notes

Chapter 1 – Welcome to College

Katherine Kendig, "How college grading is different from high school," http://college.usatoday.com/2013/05/31/how-college-grading-is-different-from-high-school/. May 31, 2013.

Chapter 2 – The Journey to Writing This Book

Sharita Forrest, Illinois News Bureau "First-semester GPA a better predictor of college success than ACT score" February 2, 2016. https://news.illinois.edu/blog/view/6367/320538.

Rachel Beckstead "College Dropout Rates and Statistics," June 29th, 2017. https://www.collegeatlas.org/college-dropout.html.

Bob Brinkmann, "10 Tips for Freshman Success in College" http://www.huffingtonpost.com/bob-brinkmann/10-tips-for-freshman-succ_b_7949320.html. August 6, 2016.

The University of Wisconsin-Platteville, "Major Differences Between High School and College," https://www.uwplatt.edu/counseling-services/major-differences-between-high-school-and-college.

Mike Bowler, "Dropouts Loom Large for Schools" Aug 19, 2009. https://www.usnews.com/education/articles/2009/08/19/dropouts-loom-large-for-schools.

Chapter 3 – Goal Setting

"Goal Setting," Assembled by the Counseling Center at Brookhaven College, http://www.scc.losrios.edu/weeklyupdate/studyskills/goal-setting/.

Marcel Schwantes, "Science Says 92 Percent of People Don't Achieve Their Goals. Here's How the Other 8 Percent Do" https://www.inc.com/marcel-schwantes/science-says-92-percent-of-people-dont-achieve-goals-heres-how-the-other-8-perce.html. Abuhamdeh, S., & Csikszentmihalyi, M. (2012). The importance of challenge for the enjoyment of intrinsically motivated, goal-directed activities. Personality and Social Psychology Bulletin, 38, 317-330.

Heather Royer, Mark Stehr, Justin Sydnor (2015) Incentives, Commitments, and Habit Formation in Exercise: Evidence from a Field Experiment with Workers at a Fortune-500 Company. American Economic Journal: Applied Economics vol. 7, no. 3, July 2015 (pp. 51-84).

Cauley, K. M., & McMillan, J. H. (2009). Formative Assessment Techniques to Support Student Motivation and Achievement. Clearing House: A Journal of Educational Strategies, Issues and Ideas, 1-6.

Chapter 4 – Small Changes… Big Impact

Br J Gen Pract, "Making health habitual: the psychology of 'habit-formation' and general practice" BJGP 2012 Dec; 62(605): 664–666 https://www.ncbi.nlm.nih.gov/pmc/articles/PMC3505409/.

Daren Hardy, *The Compound Effect,* Success Media 2010, P.10. https://www.amazon.com/Compound-Effect-Darren-Hardy/dp/159315724X/ref=sr_1_1?ie=UTF8&qid=1498858588&sr=8-1&keywords=darren+hardy.

Chapter 5 – Time Management Strategies

Brennen Hubbard, The Blue Banner, "Study finds up to 95 percent of college students procrastinate" http://thebluebanner.net/study-finds-up-to-95-percent-of-college-students-procrastinate/.

Amy Morin, "The Secret To Ending Procrastination Is Changing The Way You Think About Deadlines," September 4. 2014.https://www.forbes.com/sites/amymorin/2014/09/04/study-the-secret-to-ending-procrastination-is-changing-the-way-you-think-about-deadlines/#7f5344508d31.

Editors of Shape.com, "6 Reasons Drinking Water Helps Solve Any Problem" http://www.shape.com/healthy-eating/healthy-drinks/6-reasons-drinking-water-helps-solve-any-problem.
ADAA, "Facts" https://www.adaa.org/finding-help/helping-others/college-students/facts.

Chapter 6 - College Life is Full of Excitement and Stress

Abiola Keller et al., "Does the perception that stress affects health matter? The association with health and mortality", *Health Psychology*, September 2012.

Jeremy P. Jamieson et al., "Mind over matter: Reappraising arousal improves cardiovascular and cognitive responses to stress," *Journal of Experimental Psychology*, August 2012.

Michael J. Poulin et al., "Giving to others and the association between stress and mortality," *American Journal of Public Health*, September 2013.

Alice G. Walton, "7 Ways Meditation Can Actually Change The Brain" https://www.forbes.com/sites/alicegwalton/2015/02/09/7-ways-meditation-can-actually-change-the-brain/#1fba415f1465. Feb 9, 2015.

ADAA, "Facts" https://www.adaa.org/finding-help/helping-others/college-students/facts.

Chapter 7 – How to Get and Stay Motivated

Daisy Yuhas, "Three Critical Elements Sustain Motivation," Scientific America, November 1, 2012. https://www.scientificamerican.com/article/three-critical-elements-sustain-motivation/.

Alina Vrabie, "Dual monitor display vs. one large monitor: workplace productivity," May 28, 2014. http://blog.sandglaz.com/workspace-productivity-one-large-monitor-vs-dual-monitors/.

Dustin Wax, "The Science of Motivation," Life Hack Blog. http://www.lifehack.org/articles/featured/the-science-of-motivation.html.

Chapter 8 – Master Your Brain

Science Daily, "Neuron" https://www.sciencedaily.com/terms/neuron.htm.

Neuroscience for Kids, https://faculty.washington.edu/chudler/synapse.html.

Mayfield Brain and Spine, "Antonymy of the Brain', https://www.mayfieldclinic.com/PE-AnatBrain.htm.

"Difference Between Neurotransmitters and Hormones" May 2, 2011. http://www.differencebetween.com/difference-between-neurotransmitters-and-vs-hormones/.

Parkinson's Clinic International, "Neurotransmitters and Hormones," http://www.bbwca.com/neurotransmitters-and-hormones/.

Bryan Kolb, Robbin Gibb, and Terry Robinson, "Brain Plasticity and Behavior," Psychological Science, http://www.psychologicalscience.org/journals/cd/12_1/kolb.cfm.

Wikipedia, "Nootropic" https://en.wikipedia.org/wiki/Nootropic.

Psychology Today, "Seasonal Affective Disorder," https://www.psychologytoday.com/conditions/seasonal-affective-disorder.

Chapter 9 – Energy and Time Management

N. Lovato and L. Lack, Flinders University "Want to boost your memory and mood? Take a nap, but keep it short." https://www.sciencealert.com/want-to-boost-your-memory-and-mood-take-a-nap-but-keep-it-short. May 17, 2013.

By Christopher Ketcham for Men's Journal "How To Power Nap For All-Day Energy." http://www.huffingtonpost.com/2014/09/15/power-nap-all-day-energy_n_5798256.html.

Chapter 10 - Managing Work and Fun

Mental Health America, "Balancing Work and School, Mental Health America," http://www.mentalhealthamerica.net/balancing-work-and-school.

Carrington College, How to Handle the Stress of School and Work" October 28, 2015. http://carrington.edu/blog/carrington/how-to-handle-the-stress-of-school-and-work/.

Chapter 11 - You Can Do It

Stanford.edu, "Steve Jobs to 2005 graduates: 'Stay hungry, stay foolish'" http://news.stanford.edu/news/2005/june15/grad-061505.html.

Chapter 12 – Conclusion and Invitation

Jordan Weissmann, Slate.com, "America's Awful College Dropout Rates, in Four Charts," November 19, 2014.
http://www.slate.com/blogs/moneybox/2014/11/19/u_s_college_dropouts_rates_explained_in_4_charts.html.

Lynn O'Shaughnessy, MoneyWatch, "20 facts you didn't know about college freshmen" February 7, 2012.
http://www.cbsnews.com/news/20-facts-you-didnt-know-about-college-freshmen/.

David Leonhardt, The New York Times, "Colleges Are Failing in Graduation Rates," September 8, 2009.
http://www.nytimes.com/2009/09/09/business/economy/09leonhardt.html.

About The Author

Dennis Stemmle is the visionary force behind College Success Academy as its founder and Chief Evangelist. As a business leader and educator with over two decades of experience, Dennis brings a unique perspective that bridges the divide between the classroom and the "so-called" real world.

Dennis distills the best of the best information and strategies available for college success, mixing his street-tested principles with those of teachers, and students from around the country. Dennis is also a best-selling author, successful entrepreneur, speaker, and Adjunct Professor at The Wall College of Business Coastal Carolina University.

Follow Dennis on Instagram and Twitter at DennisStemmle and on Facebook at CollegeSuccessAcademy.

Visit Dennis Stemmle at www.CollegeSuccessAcademy.com

For readers who want more success, you can learn more success secrets at www.IwantSuccessInCollege.com.

Made in the USA
Middletown, DE
15 July 2019